MW00583273

ADOLESCENT LITERACIES AND THE GENDERED SELF

Today's youth live in the interface of the local and the global. Research is documenting how a world youth culture is developing, how global migration is impacting youth, how global capitalism is changing their economic and vocational futures, and how computer-mediated communication with the world is changing the literacy needs and identities of students. This book explores the dynamic range of literacy practices that are reconstructing gender identities in both empowering and disempowering ways and the implications for local literacy classrooms. As gendered identities become less essentialist, are more often created in virtual settings, and are increasingly globalized, literacy educators need to understand these changes in order to effectively educate their students.

The volume is organized around three themes:

* gender influences and identities in literacy and literature;
* gender influences and identities in new literacies practices; and
* gender and literacy issues and policies.

The contributing authors offer an international perspective on literacy issues and practices. This volume is an important contribution to understanding the impact of the local and the global on how today's youth are represented and positioned in literacy practices and polices within the context of 21st century global/cosmopolitan life.

Barbara J. Guzzetti is Professor, Arizona State University, New College of Interdisciplinary Arts and Sciences and also Affiliated Faculty, Mary Lou Fulton Teachers College and School for Social Transformation, Women's and Gender Studies.

Thomas W. Bean is Professor of Literacy/Reading at the University of Nevada, Las Vegas, USA and Co-Coordinator of the Doctoral Program in the Department of Teaching and Learning, College of Education.

ADOLESCENT LITERACIES AND THE GENDERED SELF

(Re)constructing Identities Through Multimodal Literacy Practices

Edited by Barbara J. Guzzetti and Thomas W. Bean

First published 2013
by Routledge
711 Third Avenue, New York, NY 10017

Simultaneously published in the UK
by Routledge
2 Park Square, Milton Park, Abingdon, Oxfordshire OX14 4RN

Routledge is an imprint of the Taylor & Francis Group, an informa business

First issued in paperback 2014

© 2013 Taylor & Francis

The right of the editors to be identified as the authors of the editorial
material, and of the authors for their individual chapters, has been asserted in
accordance with sections 77 and 78 of the Copyright, Designs and Patents
Act 1988.

All rights reserved. No part of this book may be reprinted or reproduced or
utilised in any form or by any electronic, mechanical, or other means, now
known or hereafter invented, including photocopying and recording, or in
any information storage or retrieval system, without permission in writing
from the publishers.

Trademark notice: Product or corporate names may be trademarks or registered
trademarks, and are used only for identification and explanation without
intent to infringe.

Library of Congress Cataloging-in-Publication Data
Adolescent literacies and the gendered self : (re)constructing identities
through multimodal literacy practices / edited by Barbara J. Guzzetti, Thomas
W. Bean.
p. cm.
    Includes bibliographical references and index.
1. Literacy–Social aspects–United States. 2. Literacy–Sex differences–United
States. 3. Teenagers–Books and reading–United States. 4. Gender
identity–United States. I. Guzzetti, Barbara J. II. Bean, Thomas W.
    LC151.A44 2012
    302.2'244–dc23

                                2012026847

ISBN 978-0-415-63618-6 (hbk)
ISBN 978-1-138-84231-1 (pbk)
ISBN 978-0-203-08558-5 (ebk)

Typeset in Bembo
by Keystroke, Station Road, Codsall, Wolverhampton

We dedicate this book in fond memory of Helen Harper, and in recognition of Helen's doctoral students who continue to advocate for gender and literacy practices that acknowledge and respect students' diverse identities and life trajectories. We also acknowledge the myriad ways in which Helen's scholarship impacted our thinking and informed our lines of inquiry.

CONTENTS

FOREWORD

In a relatively short time, measured by a few decades, the work on gender and literacy in education has evolved from attention to girl/boy binaries, myths and crises to more sophisticated renditions of fluid and situated gender performances and positions. It is particularly fitting that this volume was developed by Barbara Guzzetti and Tom Bean in honor of our sorely missed colleague, Helen Harper, who was among the first North American literacy researchers to examine, in rich and passionate ways, the deployment of feminist pedagogies with youth, and whose writings here and in other venues continue to push the field of gender and literacies toward increasingly critical, transcultural and global perspectives.

Those of us who work with marginalized youth are often amazed and heartened by their deft use of a range of discursive resources to render powerful cultural critiques as a form of participation and citizenship. Not long ago, a young woman participating in a Canadian youth anti-violence project sent me a short film from her website. The three-part film includes close-ups of her lip-piercing, a section in which she is ironically addressing friends about peer pressure, and a third section in which she shares images of herself in drag, along with parodies of anti-drug public service announcement warnings. In this embodied visual production, she inscribes and repositions herself in the world in playful and resistant ways in relation to larger cultural narratives of gender, providing private/public space for writing dissent on her body and in film.

The authors in this timely and exciting volume acknowledge how youth represent themselves in and through these intersecting and often competing ideologies and discourses of gender, sexuality, race, and mobility in the context of global flows of texts, information, and bodies. The authors take us through literacy classrooms, community poetry projects, popular media representations, and youth interactions in online book clubs, filmmaking, zines, virtual worlds, and social networking sites. Readers are invited into a re-examination of gender and youth culture through these varied forms and sites of literacy, popular media, and digital technology that young people are engaging in across institutional boundaries.

Indeed a strength of this book is its focus on how youth, including—and perhaps especially—otherwise marginalized youth, can and do become engaged cultural critics in private and public spaces, both local and global, and virtual and material. In these chapters, we witness how youth use new literacy landscapes to inscribe, perform, resist and reposition themselves in and against dominant and regulatory discourses. In this way, the volume makes visible the range of youth engagements with literature, popular media, and digital technologies that challenge us as educators to be more imaginative in our support of these endeavors. It also offers a range of suggestions for navigating these complex learning spaces with adolescents.

This is not to say that such representations of and by youth do not at times re-inscribe more normative identity positions. The practices described here are not presented as exemplars, as our teaching and support of youth needs to be informed by purposes and situation of the particular youth we work with; instead this work reminds us that as educators we are called upon to continually and intentionally provide flexible spaces for dialogue and critique with and among youth as a fundamental aspect of democratic citizenship. Indeed, as the chapters in this volume illustrate, youth all around the world are consuming and producing texts in creative and critical ways, constantly challenging our theorizing about youth literacies and our notions about what constitutes a lively and responsive curriculum for today's students.

Colleagues and friends of Helen, several of whom are represented here, often speak of her humor, insightfulness and, particularly, her passion for her work. This dynamic, international volume is a testament to that work and a fitting legacy. It will be of interest to educators in many settings who are supporting young people as they traverse the landscape of new literacies, media and their cultural lives.

Theresa Rogers
University of British Columbia

PREFACE

The inspiration for this edited volume has its lineage in Helen Harper's Canadian feminist scholarship, starting with her published dissertation, *Wild Words/Dangerous Desires* (Harper, 2000), and progressing through a host of other publications including *Advocacy Research in Literacy Education: Seeking Higher Ground* (Cherland & Harper, 2007). In the introduction to *Wild Words/Dangerous Desires*, Helen located what would become a lifelong interest in identity and gender issues, directly in the classroom:

> As a former high school English teacher, I am interested in school literacy practices as a site for social and personal transformation. Acts of literacy have come to be understood, not as something transposed onto our lives, but as a lived experience that can affirm or disrupt understandings of self and the world.
>
> *(Harper, 2000, p. 3)*

Helen was a graduate of the Ontario Institute for Studies in Education, University of Toronto, and faculty member at the University of Western Ontario and subsequently, the University of Nevada, Las Vegas, where she served as Co-Editor of the *Journal of Adolescent & Adult Literacy* (International Reading Association). Her work in English education, adolescent literacy, and feminist and critical cultural studies continues to influence an international body of doctoral students and faculty.

Helen, with Barbara Guzzetti, organized a conference symposium that, upon Helen's untimely passing, resulted in a desire to continue her cosmopolitan vision in this volume. The lives of youth are and will be lived out at the nexus of the local and global with a growing need to develop students' dispositions and identities as cosmopolitan world citizens. Thus, this edited volume focuses on the representation and gender positioning of youth in literacy practices within the context of 21st-century global/cosmopolitan life, heavily influenced by the accelerated movement of people, information, ideas, images and capital across permeable offline and online borders. The authors and chapters in this volume consider the dynamic array of literacy practices that rename gender identities in empowering and disempowering ways with implications for teaching youth.

This volume provides an international perspective on gender issues spanning three continents—Europe, North America, and Australia. The audience for this volume includes literacy educators and researchers, higher education faculty, classroom teachers, literacy and media specialists, communications scholars and technology educators, as well as policymakers. A secondary audience for this volume consists of others outside of education concerned with issues of gender justice and social justice. In addition, this volume can serve as a text for preservice and inservice classes exploring gender issues.

Organization

The book is organized in three parts: Gender Influences and Identities in Literacy and Literature; Gender Influences and Identities in New Literacies Practices; and Gender and Literacy: Issues and Policies.

Part I Gender Influences and Identities in Literacy and Literature

In Chapter 1, "Outside Interests and Literate Practices as Contexts for Increasing Engagement and Critical Reading for Adolescent Boys," Bill Brozo offers specific examples from classrooms where teachers are using social media to get boys interested in reading. In Chapter 2, "Taking Patriarchy to Task: Youth, YouTube, and Young Adult Literature," Karen Krasny considers a feminist approach to literacy instruction aimed at political advocacy. In Chapter 3, "Masculinity and Portrayals of African American Boys in Young Adult Literature: A Critical Deconstruction and Reconstruction of this Genre," authors Tom Bean and Theodore Ransaw explore the intersection of African American young adult literature and masculine theory, offering specific readings for teachers. Chapter 4, "One World: Understanding the Discourse of Benevolent Girlhood through Critical Media Literacy" by Elizabeth Marshall and Özlem Sensoy focuses on the Cheetah Girls, a girl band constructed and made popular by the Disney franchise and related film, *One World*, emphasizing girls in traditional helping roles.

Part II Gender Influences and Identities in New Literacies Practices

In Chapter 5, "The Image You Choose is the Avatar You Use: Re-Thinking Gender in New Literacies," British scholar Guy Merchant offers readers three cases of youth discussing their gendered representations in social media sites, the author's use of 3D virtual worlds in classrooms, and the self-representation of digital leaders in a collaborative school literacy project. In Chapter 6, "Girls' Zines as a Global Literacy Practice: Stories of Resistance and Representation," Barbara Guzzetti draws attention to the shared issues and concerns raised by young women across the globe in enacting their identities as females in the 21st century. Three data sources of zines collected from the author's international travels inform the chapter and offer readers a vision of how girls use zines to regender and empower themselves. In Chapter 7, "Literacies, Identities and Gender: Reframing Girls in Digital Worlds, " Cheryl McLean illustrates how immigrant youth literacy online practices negotiate cultural and gendered transnational identities. Chapter 8, "Entrepreneurship Education and Gendered Discursive Practices" features Donna Alvermann's 8-month study of a 10th-grade African American student's use of multimodal texts and social networking sites to gain a sense of self-efficacy in literacy. In Chapter 9, "A Cautionary Tale: Online School Book Clubs Are No Panacea for African American Adolescent Females' Coming to Voice," Benita Dillard presents the experiences of three adolescent African American females in online spaces of chat rooms, emails, and VoiceThread as they discussed their lived experiences in response to young adult literature selections. Chapter 10, "Gender, Multimodal Practices and Global Citizenship in Rural Settings," Carla Meyer and Leslie Susan Cook consider how youth from sparsely populated areas are participating in cosmopolitan communities through their use of 21st-century online mediums. In Chapter 11, "A New Look at Girls, Gaming, and Literacies," Elisabeth Hayes explores the new literacies involved in girls' gaming practices in light of the changing landscape of games and gaming communities, with more girls engaged in global gaming networks.

Part III Gender and Literacy: Issues and Policies

In Chapter 12, "The Girl Citizen-Reader: Gender and Literacy Education for 21st-Century Citizenship," Judith Dunkerly and Helen Harper consider how gender and literacy education might be reconfigured to support girls' global citizenship with a particular focus on two agencies that support this move-ment. Chapter 13, "Who Will "Save the Boys"? (Re)Examining a Panic for Underachieving Boys" provides Michael Kehler's survey and critical analysis of global policies in response to the alleged boy crisis in reading achievement. In Chapter 14, "Inventing Masculinity: Young Black Males, Literacy, and Tears," David Kirkland explores the historical and contemporary role of tears as a metaphor that deconstructs hegemonic masculinity in poetry and other creative forms that expand African American male positioning. In Chapter 15, "Gendered Subjectivities in Online Spaces: The Significance of Genderqueer Youth Writing Practices in a Global Time," Jennifer Ingrey examines the flow of representations of identity through multimedia communications technology as they relate to the positioning or transgender and genderqueer youth.

In summary, we invite the reader to explore the multimodal literacy practices and contemporary gender identities global youth are actively constructing, particularly as digital natives well versed in social media practices that link vast geographic distances and diverse cultures. As Helen Harper argued:

> It is possible to be a local resident and a transnational or global worker; a national, and multi-national citizen; a local consumer/producer and a global consumer/producer; a community member fluent in the local literacy practices, but also a global worker/citizen/consumer who has or needs multiliterate, multilingual, multimodal skills and abilities. At the very least, the movement of information, ideas, images, capital and people insures that community-based members' lives are lived out and affected by diverse global forces, whether they are conscious of it or not.
>
> *(Harper et al., 2010, p. 4)*

We hope that you find the chapters in this volume helpful in your teaching and research related to gender and identity.

Barbara J. Guzzetti
Thomas W. Bean

References

Cherland, M.R. & Harper, H.J. (2007). *Advocacy research in literacy education: Seeking higher ground.* Mahwah, NJ: Lawrence Erlbaum.

Harper, H.J. (2000). *Wild words/Dangerous desires: High school girls & feminist avant-garde writing.* New York: Peter Lang.

Harper, H.J., Bean, T.W., & Dunkerly, J. (2010). Cosmopolitanism, globalization, and the field of adolescent literacy. *Canadian and International Education, 39*(3), 1–13.

PART I

Gender Influences and Identities in Literacy and Literature

1

OUTSIDE INTERESTS AND LITERATE PRACTICES AS CONTEXTS FOR INCREASING ENGAGEMENT AND CRITICAL READING FOR ADOLESCENT BOYS

William G. Brozo

In 2011, a Schott Foundation study found that only 47% of African American males graduate from high school. Those victimized by this national scandal are too often doomed to a grinding cycle of poverty, unemployment, and other economic, social, and personal setbacks. Among the galaxy of causes for these alarming numbers of dropouts for boys of color, one cause is almost assuredly related to insufficient literacy ability (Brozo, 2010; Tatum, 2005, 2008; Vacca, 2008). Regardless of the ultimate career and life choice a boy might pursue, the tool all male youth need to become effective problem solvers, flexible decision makers, and critical thinkers is skillful reading ability. Skilled readers are far more likely to be successful at home and in the workplace than their unskilled peers (Center for Workforce Preparation, 2004; Sum et al., 2007). Adolescent males with low levels of literacy will be at a great and increasing disadvantage in today's global economy. In a world driven by information and knowledge, their skill deficiencies will limit access to the full range of opportunities enjoyed by their more literate peers (Hofstetter et al., 1999). Thus, the quality of literacy competence boys develop as young adults will impact their competence in personal, occupational, and community life as adults.

I make the case in this chapter that male youth increase their chances of developing the literate abilities and dispositions necessary for full participation as global citizens if they're exposed to and have meaningful and enjoyable literacy and learning experiences around texts of interest. I call for schools to come to know and learn to value adolescent boys' interests and literate practices beyond the school walls. I assert that these texts and the literate practices boys already engage in outside of school can be honored in school to capture boys' unique imaginations, sustain their attention, and lead to more thoughtful reading and writing.

Situating school-based instruction within authentic language contexts for adolescent boys means honoring their discourses and media. Adolescents are on the vanguard of a new literacy revolution consuming, reconfiguring, and creating ever-evolving ways of exploiting new media to suit their varied communication purposes and identity needs (Alvermann & Wilson, 2007; Vasudevan, 2006). As active participants in the "mediasphere" (O'Brien, 2001), male youth are using and creating forms of discourse that should be acknowledged and appreciated in school settings. Upper-grades teachers who are turning increasingly to new media are discovering that they are inherently motivating to many male youth (Weinstein, 2002). Teachers in all subject areas are exploring multimedia possibilities for engaging listless male learners (O'Brien & Dubbels, 2003; O'Brien et al., 2007) and connecting alternative text sources with traditional texts to increase male students' understanding and utility of content (Brozo, 2007).

Drawing on scenes of classroom life, I document how teachers across the United States are making room for boys' out-of-school interests and literacies resulting in numerous opportunities for engaged, purposeful, and critical reading (Brozo, 2010; Coles & Hall, 2001). In these scenes, teachers are motivating boys by channeling their diverse communicative practices into identity-affirming and competence-building reading and writing events for them (Unrau & Schlackman, 2006).

Popular Media in the Classroom

Creative and responsive teachers find ways to honor adolescent male youths outside-of-school media while bridging them to the concepts and information in the classroom. An obvious source for enlivening school-based learning for boys is popular media and music (Knabb, 2003; Pailliotet, 2003). It makes good sense to find as many linkages as possible between the images and music with which boys are familiar and topics under study in the classroom (Morrell, 2002).

Music, as a medium of identity construction for boys, is a very viable alternative text form under-exploited by most teachers (Newman, 2005; Williams, 2004). Scaffolding for new understandings means working with what boys bring to the classroom, including their interest in and knowledge of popular music (Dimitriadis, 2001; Hill, 2009; Morrell & Duncan-Andrade, 2002).

Teaching Word Families with Hip-Hop

Derrick is a reading teacher in a large suburban middle-school. His 3rd period class is comprised of mostly boys who are reading well below their grade placement, in some cases as much as three to five years. Derrick knows that for students with a history of reading and learning failure they need text encounters and experiences that increase engagement and agency. One way he does this is by tapping into their media and music for teaching aspects of language and composition.

For instance, when preparing his class for a study of word families, he first found out what his male students had programmed on their phones and other portable music devices. He then tracked down the lyrics from some of these songs and raps and found they were comprised of a variety of words that could be studied as families and then could be used as models for other similar words in school texts and in their own writing. With his students' own music as text for learning word families, Derrick noted most students, especially the boys in class, were eager to participate in the lessons, remembered more content, and gave more thoughtful responses.

When studying the "ch" and "ck" consonant digraphs, Derrick invited students to bring in lyrics with these elements. As long as the song or rap lyrics met acceptable school standards (no profanity, excessive violence, or degrading messages about women and girls), students were allowed to work with them in their analysis. With a partner, first students were to create a t-chart listing all the words that had either the "ch" or "ck" element. One pair of African American boys brought in and analyzed the rap lyric "I Love to Give You Light" by Snoop Dogg. The boys found many words with the word family elements (see Table 1.1).

TABLE 1.1 T-chart with words from "I Love to Give You Light" with /ch/ and /ck/ sounds

ch	*ck*
such	background
preach	jackers
chuuch	glock
teachin'	block
watchin'	locked
each	black
preachin'	
reach	
beach	
child	

Derrick then directed the students to generate new words with the /ch/ and /ck/ sounds and add these to their t-chart. The pair with Snoop Dogg's rap lyrics added "catch," "match," "reach," and "bunch" to the left-column words, and "socks," "locker," "backpack," and "stick" to the right-column words. Each pair of students completed activities with the song lyrics they had brought to class to analyze.

Using their new words, students were then asked to write lyrics based on the genre of music they analyzed. The lyrics had to contain the new words they generated to match the /ch/ and /ck/ sounds. Thus, the boys working with the Snoop Dogg rap wrote their own. While one kept rhythm on his desk top, the other one read the rap:

> I put my *socks* in my *backpack* when I go to school.
> I put my *backpack* in my *locker* or I look like a fool.
> I get my *socks* from my backpack when I go to gym.
> Where I *catch* the ball then *stick* it in the rim.

With this approach, Derrick witnessed how using song lyrics of favorite musical artists for doing word study not only generated enthusiasm but also translated into genuine learning. The students increased their ability to recognize many of the same words and those with the same word family elements in their own and their classmates' compositions, and as they read stories and other texts. This level of application and transfer occurred because Derrick eliminated barriers between outside-of-school interests and youth media and the literacy needs of his students.

Teaching Allusion Using Youth Media

Alejandro decided to administer a questionnaire to the 10th graders in his general English class at the beginning of the school year to try to gain insights into ways of structuring learning that would be more appealing to them. Two of the most common suggestions that came from his male students were: (a) more choices and options, particularly in the ways they are assessed, and (b) being able to use the computer and Internet for class assignments. With this information in hand, Alejandro created a range of different ways students could demonstrate under-standing of newly learned content with digital media.

One striking example of how Alejandro took advantage of his male students' input was the approach he used to teach about allusion in literature. Allusion is a difficult literary device for students to appreciate, because it's a reference in a literary work to a person, place, or thing in history or another work of literature. Allusions are often indirect or brief references to characters or events, but if readers don't know the events and characters to which an author alludes, then the allusion loses its impact.

To help sensitize his students to this literary device and bring them to appreciate its significance, Alejandro's gave the class its initial exposure to allusion through a YouTube video clip of *Shrek 2*, a popular animated film for youth. The 3-minute clip includes several visual allusions to other films and film characters, both real and animated, with the song "My Boy Lollypop" as the soundtrack. As the clip played, Alejandro asked students to note any images that referenced other movies or movie characters, and then held a discussion afterward. This visual approach, using media from his students' everyday lives, proved quite successful, as they were able to identify several allusions in the video. Alejandro was especially pleased with the involvement and participation of his male students in this activity.

Next, Alejandro guided his students through a class blog he had established. He indicated where they were to make entries and respond to their classmates. His assignment to them was to find examples of allusion in their own media—books, films, TV, games, music, etc.—and post it on the blog with an explanation of the allusion. Each student was required to post two examples on the blog and write two entries in response to their classmates.

Alejandro was surprised and pleased to find the range and depth of student responses to his assignment when he checked the site a couple of days later. What pleased him most were the contributions from his boys. They were at a level of sophistication and reflected a level of involvement he was sure he wouldn't have seen if the assignment had been framed in a more traditional way, as these three examples attest:

"Evan"

The avant garde music group Mr. Bungle modified the Warner Brothers' logo into their own creation. By simply flipping and turning their record's label (Warner Brothers), they made an already existing logo into something brand spanking new. This is an allusion to the band's label, so it is kind of like a self-promoting allusion.

"Jung-Hee"

My allusion is from the anime *Lucky Star* (which no one has probably heard of, but is the only one I can think of at the moment). In one of the episodes, the main character, Konata, cosplays [dresses up] as a character from another anime, Haruhi from *The Melancholy of Haruhi Suzumiya* at a cosplay café. The function of this allusion, in a way, is self-promotion because the writers of *Lucky Star* also wrote *The Melancholy of Haruhi Suzumiya*.

"Fareed"

I found one from *Family Guy*:

http://www.youtube.com/watch?v=AMAA0dfZRsU&feature=related

This is an allusion to *The Ring*, like how when you watch the cursed video in the movie *The Ring*, you'll die. In *Family Guy*, the cursed video is *The Simpsons*, which is their rival. And if you watch it, they're basically saying *The Simpsons* is bad for you.

From here, Alejandro transitioned his class into looking for and uncovering allusions in traditional print texts, which they did with far greater success than they had in previous years. With this assignment, Alejandro was able to take advantage of his students' competencies with media and literacies outside of school to achieve his goal of motivating reluctant and disinterested male youth to read and respond on a more thoughtful level to required texts in his classroom.

Community/Work-Based Learning as Authentic Language Contexts

Learning that puts students directly to work on community problems that are often in need of volunteers and require imaginative solutions can be a powerful impetus for developing language and literacy skills for boys (Brozo, 2010). It has been demonstrated that participants in school-sponsored, community- and work-based learning activities enjoy numerous academic, personal, and social benefits (Billig, 2000). These benefits include increased student engagement (Yates & Youniss, 1998), overall scholastic improvement (Skinner & Chapman, 1999), attainment of higher-level thinking skills (Eyler & Giles, 1999), greater interpersonal competence (Melchior & Ballis 2001), and exploration of various career pathways (Furco, 2001). Given these benefits, community- and work-based learning experiences would appear to present teachers and students real-world application of skills while increasing civic pride and academic achievement.

Applying Principles of Room Design in Building Homes for Habitat

For Chauncey's building trades students, giving time to assist professional draftsmen with room design of Habitat for Humanity homes and help build them was just what was needed to enliven his class. Talking about design concepts for sleeping, service, and living areas and looking at examples of room flow is one thing, applying these ideas to actual home design is quite another. Always on the lookout for opportunities to move his lessons from the hypothetical to the possible, Chauncey was quick to offer the services of his class after responding to an announcement in the paper of a Habitat project commencing soon that was seeking local labor. Virtually every boy's hand shot into the air when he asked if there was any interest in volunteering.

Chauncey made arrangements for the project architect to speak to his class about the work to be done and the ways the students might contribute to room design. The guest speaker explained that there were to be built five houses in different locations throughout town. Each one would follow a common general plan while allowing for some small variability depending upon the lot size and grading. He then left the class with a copy of blueprints, asking them to look for ways of improving room flow in ways that maximize living areas in the small houses. Chauncey expanded on this challenge by also requesting students work in design groups to (a) research Habitat for Humanity's history and mission, as well as the housing needs of the poor in the city, (b) make structural drawings to scale using appropriate terms and symbols, and (c) write and present a brief PowerPoint report that identified the architectural problem, a plan for solving the problem and blueprints for executing the solution.

In the following weeks, Chauncey's students worked on this assignment while donating a few hours per week assisting in the construction of the houses. He handled all of the permissions and liability forms and was able to use a school van to take students to and from the building sites two days per week during the 90-minute class period. With a tremendous sense of pride, students, in their hardhats, joined the other volunteers in the myriad tasks assigned by the job foreman. While on site, they were also able to share their ideas with and ask questions of the architect, who offered helpful recommendations and insights. He was invited back to class for the student PowerPoint presentations, where he gave additional helpful critiques.

Increasing Health Awareness with ICT Tools

Students in Mr. Aldape's health careers class are participating in an experimental GED program that allows them to attend school in the morning and gain valuable work experiences in the afternoon. Students are provided integrated reading, writing, math, and GED test preparation instruction within the study of various vocational areas. Every day, students are engaged in activities involving writing as meaningful communication, using information and communications technologies (ICTs) for research and production, reading for working, and developing test-taking strategies. Mr. Aldape's students are not required to sit in desks and rows but are given freedom of movement to pursue the completion of assignments tailored to their unique career interests and workplace experiences.

Manolo is in the class because of his interest in seeking a career in the health field. His assignments are applied to the content and texts of his work placement in a doctor's clinic. Thus, he practices the split-page technique for taking notes by separating the major concepts from the significant details and recording them in a two-column format, using content from brochures and manuals available to employees in the clinic. Various office brochures, such as "Counter Effects of Aspirin with Other Drugs," "Life Expectancy is Going Up," and "Preoperative Precautions," provide Manolo the practice material for constructing appropriate pre-questions as guides to reading. With this same material, Mr. Aldape models reading strategies such as previewing, self-questioning, determining word meanings from context, gisting, organizing information into graphic displays, and checking for understanding. As each of these literacy processes is modeled, he immediately elicits similar behaviors from Manolo and his classmates. For example, with a passage about deep vein thrombophlebitis, they work side-by-side, moving through the text in a model-elicit process, thinking aloud about content and processes for organizing and understanding it. When they come upon the word "anticoagulant," Mr. Aldape draws attention to the other words in the sentence that refer to treatments involving thinning the blood, which helps Manolo understand it. Later, when Manolo encounters the word "vascular," he is able to use the words and sentences around it to determine that it is related to the veins.

The approach of tying literacy strategies to workplace content creates a highly engaged atmosphere of learning for Manolo and his classmates in the health careers course. He becomes a more interested and participatory learner than he had been as a student in the general high school curriculum. This is most apparent during the development of a work-based project as one of the major assignments of Mr. Aldape's class. The project's goal is to help students think critically about their work settings and how to better inform and serve the intended clientele or consumer. They have to create an actual "product" using ICT tools and make it available to employers as a demonstration of their meaningful and creative contributions to the business.

For his project Manolo decides to help make the office waiting room a more consumer-friendly environment. In the month since he started work, he has been called upon to visit with and help relax unaccompanied seniors in the waiting room and patient rooms. And, with his fluent Spanish, he facilitates the nurse practitioners and the two office doctors when communicating with the growing number of Latino/a patients. During these activities, the idea occurs to him of creating an interactive touch screen, that operates much like an automated teller machine (ATM), for Spanish-speaking clients. It will answer basic questions for them about checking in, payments and co-payments, government and privately funded medical insurance, preventive health, and more. Pulling information on these topics from brochures and forms along with touchFLO technology, Manolo, with Mr. Aldape's help, creates a colorful, interactive computer screen in Spanish accompanied by photos and video. One can read or, for those with reading or vision problems, listen to directions and information by touching labeled buttons on the screen. One of the buttons is for frequently asked questions and answers, which Manolo obtained through interviews with the office manager and the doctors, then edited. Hyperlinks to short relevant video are built into the options.

The office doctors allow Manolo to set up two LCD screens in the waiting room and bright flyers in Spanish invited users to give them a try. On the table next to the screens are response forms, also written in Spanish, in order to gather feedback from users on problems with the system and suggestions for improving it. When Latino/a patients arrive, Manolo guides them to the screens to make certain they feel comfortable using the program. He shows them where to press buttons for information about the clinic's services as well as insurance and methods of payment. Patients catch on quickly and seem to have little trouble maneuvering through the interactive program.

Implications for Literacy Educators

The four vignettes in this chapter make clear that boys can become engaged readers and learners and independent knowledge seekers when they perceive what they are learning to be personally meaningful and relevant to their lives and futures. Creating contexts for learning that are engaging for boys begins with an understanding of their outside-of-school literate practices and interests. With this knowledge, teachers can plan learning experiences in academic settings that honor boys' media as well as their identities and aspirations.

References

Alvermann, D.E. & Wilson, A.A. (2007). Redefining adolescent literacy instruction. In B.J. Guzzetti (Ed.), *Literacy for the new millennium* (Volume 3, pp. 3–20). Westport, CT: Praeger.

Anderson, K.A., Howard, K.E., & Graham, A. (2008). Reading achievement, suspensions, and African American males in middle school. *Reading Achievement & Suspensions, 2*(2), 43–63.

Billig, S.H. (2000). Research on K–12 school-based service-learning: The evidence builds. *Phi Delta Kappan, 81*, 658–664.

Brozo, W.G. (2007). Helping boys find entry points to lifelong reading: Book clubs and other strategies for struggling adolescent males (pp. 304–318). In J. Lewis & G. Moorman (Eds.), *Adolescent literacy instruction: Policies and promising practices*. Newark, DE: International Reading Association.

Brozo, W.G. (2010). *To be a boy, to be a reader: Engaging teen and preteen boys in active literacy* (2nd ed.). Newark, DE: International Reading Association.

Center for Workforce Preparation. (2004). *A chamber guide to improving workplace literacy*. Washington, DC: U.S. Chamber of Commerce.

Coles, M. & Hall, C. (2001). Boys, books and breaking boundaries: Developing literacy in and out of school. In W. Martino & B. Meyenn (Eds.), *What about the boys? Issues of masculinity in schools*. Buckingham, UK: Open University Press.

Dimitriadis, G. (2001). "In the clique": Popular culture, constructions of place, and the everyday lives of urban youth. *Anthropology & Education Quarterly, 32*, 29–51.

Eyler, J. & Giles, D. (1999). *Where's the learning in service-learning?* San Francisco: Jossey-Bass Publishers.

Furco, A. (2001). Is service-learning really better than community service? A study of high school service program outcomes. In A. Furco & S.H. Billig (Eds.), *Service-learning: The essence of the pedagogy*. Greenwich, CT: Information Age Publishers.

Hill, M.L. (2009). Wounded healing: Forming a storytelling community in hip-hop lit. *Teachers College Record, 111*(1), 248–293

Hofstetter, C., Sticht, T., & Hofstetter, C. (1999). Knowledge, literacy and power. *Communication Research, 26*, 58–80.

Hughes-Hassell, S. & Rodge, P. (2007). The leisure reading habits of urban adolescents. *Journal* of Adolescent & Adult Literacy, *51*(1), 22–33.

Kirkland, D.E. (2011). Books like clothes: Engaging young black men with reading. *Journal of Adolescent and Adult Literacy, 55*(3), 199–208.

Knabb, M. (2003). Rapping to review: A novel strategy to engage students and summarize course material. *Advances in Physiological Education, 27*, 157–159.

Melchior, A. & Ballis, L.N. (2001). Impact of service-learning on civic attitudes and behaviors of middle and high school youth: Findings from three national evaluations. In A. Furco & S.H. Billig (Eds.), *Service-learning: The essence of the pedagogy*. Greenwich, CT: Information Age Publishers.

Morrell, E. (2002). Toward a critical pedagogy of popular culture: Literacy development among urban youth. *Journal of Adolescent and Adult Literacy, 46*(1), 72–77.

Morrell, E. & Duncan-Andrade, J. (2002). What do they learn in school? Using hip-hop as a bridge between youth culture and canonical poetry texts. In J. Mahiri (Ed.), *What They Don't Learn in School: Literacy in the Lives of Urban Youth*. New York: Peter Lang.

Newman, M. (2005). Rap as literacy: A genre analysis of hip-hop ciphers. *Interdisciplinary Journal for the Study of Discourse, 25*, 399–436.

O'Brien, D.G. (2001). "At-risk" adolescents: Redefining competence through the multiliteracies of intermediality, visual arts, and representation. *Reading Online, 4*(11). Available: http://www.readingonline.org/newliteracies/lit_Index.asp?HREF=/new literacies/obrien/index.html

O'Brien, D. & Dubbels, B. (2003). Reading-to-learn: From print to new digital media and new literacies. Naperville, IL: National Central Regional Educational Laboratory. http://vgalt.com/2010/05/13/reading-to-learn-fromprint-to-new-digital-media-and-new literacies/

O'Brien, D., Beach, R., & Scharber, C. (2007). "Struggling" middle schoolers: Engagement and literate competence in a reading writing intervention class. *Reading Psychology, 28*, 51–73.

Pailliotet, A.W. (2003). Integrating media and popular-culture literacy with content reading. In R.C. Richards & M.C. McKenna (Eds.), *Integrating multiple literacies in K–8 classrooms: Case commentaries and practical applications*, pp. 172–189. Mahwah, NJ: Lawrence Erlbaum.

Schott Foundation for Public Education. (2011). *50 state report on Black males and education.* Retrieved February 22, 2012, from www.blackboysreport.org

Skinner, R. & Chapman, C. (1999). *Service-learning and community service in K–12 public schools.* Washington, DC: National Center for Education Statistics.

Sum, A., Khatiwada, I., McLaughlin, J., & Tobar, P. (2007). *The educational attainment of the nation's young black men and their recent labor market experiences: What can be done to improve their future labor market and educational prospects.* Boston: Center for Labor Market Studies, Northeastern University.

Tatum, A. (2005). *Teaching reading to Black adolescent males: Closing the achievement gap.* Portland, ME: Stenhouse Publishers.

Tatum, A. (2008). Toward a more anatomically complete model of literacy instruction: A focus on African American male adolescents and texts. *Harvard Educational Review, 78*(1), 155–180.

Unrau, N. & Schlackman, J. (2006). Motivation and its relationship with reading achievement in an urban middle school. *Journal of Educational Research, 100*(2), 81–101.

Vacca, J.S. (2008). Crime can be prevented if schools teach juvenile offenders to read. *Child and Youth Services Review, 30*, 1055–1062.

Vasudevan, L. (2006). Making known differently: Engaging visual modalities as spaces to author new selves. *E-Learning, 3*(2), 207–216.

Weinstein, S. (2002). The writing on the wall: Attending to students' self-motivated literacy. *English Education, 35*(1), 21–45.

Williams, B.T. (2004). Boys may be boys, but do they have to read and write that way? *Journal of Adolescent & Adult Literacy, 47*, 510–515.

Yates, M. & Youniss, J. (1998). Community service and political identity development in adolescence. *Journal of Social Issues, 54*, 95–112.

2

TAKING PATRIARCHY TO TASK

Youth, YouTube, and Young Adult Literature

Karen A. Krasny

As a friend who could always see beyond the surface of things, and as a feminist scholar whose critical projects signaled the need to dismantle gendered hierarchies, Helen Harper, in whose memory this book is dedicated, was one colleague who didn't need convincing that patriarchy is very much with us. The implementation of progressive gender politics presents a formidable challenge for literacy educators. A recent social networking phenomenon immediately left me imagining what Helen and her students would have had to say in response.

Since its YouTube launch on March 5, 2012, and the time I sat down a week later to write the final draft of this chapter on March 12, 2012, Jason Russell's social media campaign to attract attention to the crimes against humanity committed by Joseph Kony and his "Lord's Resistance Army" in Northern Uganda and Southern Sudan had registered more than 72,000,000 hits. I was first alerted to *Kony 2012* (Invisible Children, 2012, http://www.youtube.com/watch?v=Y4MnpzG5Sqc) by my son, who had been analyzing the 30-minute YouTube video gone viral as part of a paper he was writing for an undergraduate course in *Business and Society* that engages students in deconstructing advertising. Russell's video employs sophisticated documentary film techniques to create a highly fetishized image of activism designed to establish truth and an ethical sense of responsibility similar to the way advertisers successfully mine "ribbon" campaigns for breast cancer and other causes to sell their product. The debate over the financial transparency of Russell's charity, the ambiguity of the campaign's agenda, Russell's gloss of the political and historical complexities underlying the conditions in Uganda and elsewhere that would contribute to the rise of Joseph Kony and the L.R.A., and his skillfully creative manipulation of interviews past and present will likely continue to generate worldwide commentary. This commentary is expected to occur through online blogs, counter campaigns, and international news reports for some time to come, matched only perhaps by interest surrounding the more recent news of Russell's arrest for indecent and unruly behavior in San Diego traffic.

What immediately struck me within the first several minutes of Russell's *Kony 2012* YouTube video, however, long before I got to the hauntingly beautiful image of the child soldier set against the expensively produced 3D background, was the blatantly obvious and unapologetic patriarchal and colonizing overtones (which in the mind of this writer have come to represent one and the same) that ideologically frame the call to action motivating millions to pay attention, mostly young adults. Through a personal narrative structured around Russell's relationship with his young son Gavin, and a professed desire to make the world a better place for children everywhere, "we," that is to say, mostly white, young, male North American viewers, are supposed to collectively aspire to do our part by being more like Russell. In case viewers lose sight of Russell as the central focus Gavin reminds us at the conclusion of the video to whom we bestow our attention declaring, "I'm going to be like you, Dad." But, how does the video position Gavin's mother? The video opens with Russell's wife giving birth to their son. As film editor, Mary Patricia O'Meara (personal communication, March 13, 2012) points out, we see the mother strictly as an object here, "encased in medical equipment, completely immobile and shrouded in cloth, not even able to watch the birth of her son" (personal communication). Through tears, we listen to her say, "I can hear him!" Russell's hand is on her cheek, a sign of comfort and control to be sure, but signals to viewers that as far as this father-son narrative is concerned her job is more or less done. Those watching closely will note that Russell's wife is not the only female member of the family deemed immaterial for the purposes of this narrative construction. Russell appears to have a daughter as O'Meara is able to stop frame and zoom in to show me that she appears in a shot where we see Russell and his son, Gavin playfully wrestling together on a bed, conveniently obscured by Russell's arm that is extended toward his son.

Establishing the father-son dyadic relationship proves essential to structuring the patriarchal subtext that effectively co-opts the voice of Ugandans and in particular, the narrative of the former child soldier, Jacob. We are first introduced to Jacob and the plight of Kony's child soldiers through Russell's Facebook wall. Relying heavily on images of social networking to engage youth and young adults, Russell subsumes Jacob's narrative within the context of his own personal timeline, selecting the sound bites and images that build his story of international activist extraordinaire and American super father. Photos appear of Russell with Jacob at what may be a ball game and at SeaWorld. Shortly after scanning Russell's Facebook timeline, the video shifts viewers' attention from Russell's "paternal" relationship to Jacob toward America's relationship to Uganda. The "father knows best" motif can be read in Russell's campaign posters and promotional materials branding the Ugandan cause (which so many Ugandans have vehemently protested no longer exists, at least not in the way that it is portrayed here) with a bi-partisan

Democratic Donkey and Republican elephant. It is at this point that this carefully constructed patriarchal narrative becomes a colonizing parable.

That Russell is so adept at banking on patriarchal capitalism to advance his campaign is no surprise, given that we live in a world in which media continues to reconcile girls and women to the domestic, nurturing, and maternal. Perhaps nowhere has this been more successfully exploited than in the Swiffer cleaning products' "Dysfunctional Relationships" campaign (http://www.youtube.com/watch?v=dZYt5L56gss&feature=relmfu) (http://www.youtube.com/watch?v=M24TR6ULIb0&feature=relmfu). Among the many constant reminders from advertisers to girls and women to curb their aspirations and not to get too far ahead of themselves, Swiffer's commercials would grant women agency and voice only insofar as they can don a "power suit" and put their broom on trial or take down their mop in political debate. The Advertising Research Foundation (2011, http://www.thearf.org/ogilvy-11-winners.php) touts the campaign as a "partnership between smart research and insight-based advertising that has helped drive the continued success of one of the biggest new brand successes of the decade." The ads are unabashedly targeted at the "'The Driven Caretaker' . . . a woman who has a high level of involvement in taking care of her home and family. She believes it is her duty to make her home as clean, hygienic and orderly as she can for her family," antiseptically impossible standards that the magic of television has taught her are achievable.

Returning to the Kony 2012 video, in yet another demonstration of patriarchal controlled discourse, the short sequence that highlights the female response to the celebrated announcement from President Barack Obama of the decision to send American troops to Uganda depicts a smartly dressed African American spokeswoman, as the *unnamed* "woman behind the man" endorsing the decision on MSNBC's *The Rachel Maddow Show*. The American interview clip is closely followed by a response from Jolly Okot, Country Director of *Invisible Children*, the organization founded by Russell, who lends a rare Ugandan and female voice to the video, but whose authority is seriously undermined as she is reduced to tears midsentence to project in this brief moment another damsel in distress dressed in business attire grateful for her avenging hero. At least this time, the hero does not arrive in the form of a stylized mop. Lest one dare to hope that Gavin will be socialized into a world more sensitive to patriarchal gender configurations and responsive to the subjugation of women, Russell's precociously enlightened son bursts that bubble by employing what appears to be the new Action Movie FX app which allows iPhone users to apply special effects on top of iPhone video as he takes misogynistic aim to "explode" the ample behind of an unsuspecting woman in a supermarket.

The question of whether or not Russell's social media campaign is genuinely aimed at bringing Kony to justice and at putting an end to atrocities in Northern Uganda and Southern Sudan or whether it is, as some claim, a smokescreen for other agendas is not my focus here, and no doubt readers will have already formed their own opinion. My primary aim in introducing Russell's *Kony 2012* YouTube video is to make literacy educators aware of the need for engaged and ongoing inquiry into how oral, visual, and written texts rearticulate and sustain hegemonic privilege and patriarchal entitlement. For example, in this case of the *Kony 2012* video, how does fatherhood as a central and unifying subtext contribute to the plausibility of Russell's campaign? How does Russell's image as the socially conscious young father elicit viewer's affective engagement and potential financial contribution to his project? How might Russell have presented his campaign without relying on a patriarchal narrative? And perhaps, most importantly, how are we, the audience, complicit in sustaining patriarchy as a hegemonic discourse?

Paradoxically, the video, which undeniably moved a global youth army to action, alerted me to the need to identify works that enable students, both girls and boys, to enact their gendered subjectivities in *collective* and *political* ways that resist oppression by seeking liberation from patriarchal scripts. To this end, I suggest that literacy scholarship on young adult (YA) literature might entertain a move from the poststructuralist emphasis on individual subjectivities to a material feminist approach with its focus on collective change through a politics of subjectivity. At the same time, I want to make clear that critical literacy practices or those practices aimed at challenging taken-for-granted gendered relations, which include close readings/viewings to produce textual analysis and reader response, are of limited value without an integrated approach that effectively takes into account the multiple discourses that constitute the socially mediated context in which students acquire knowledge both in and out of school, online and off.

Children's literature scholars, librarians, and teachers alike, have long looked toward YA fiction to provide children and adolescents the imaginative spaces to explore gendered options for themselves that resist the overly determined male/female binaries of hetero-patriarchal norms. Roberta Seelinger Trites (1997) has written substantially on works that provide "an important counterbalance to traditional depictions of female passivity" (p. 47) claiming twentieth-century narratives that illustrate female investment in subjectivity tend to focus on the protagonist's path to vocalization. Elaine Showalter (1981) calls for a feminist critique that would focus on women's access to language. "The problem," as she sees it, "is not that language is insufficient to express women's consciousness but that women have been denied the full resources of language and have been forced into silence, euphemism, or circumlocution" (p. 193). Trites points to Cassie, the 10-year-old protagonist of Mildred B. Taylor's (1981) *Let the Circle be Unbroken* who experiences her unique form of speechlessness in response to her confusion over her identity or difference from others within her rural Mississippi community during the Depression. Cassie presents an all too familiar example of an articulate girl willing to voice her opinion, but subject to constant reminders from those around her to keep silent. Trites demonstrates that Cassie's identity is eventually tied both to a recognition of "the sources of her marginalization" (p. 51) and of a growing awareness of her place in a dialogic existence in which her voice can have an effect on others and in turn, the opinions and responses of others will affect her subjectivity.

The poststructural implication is that reading books that focus on individual subjectivities, that is to say, interpretations unique to a person experiencing them can be a transformative experience of political and social significance for the reader. For example, Bronwyn Davies (1989) argues that literature's liberatory potential lies in furnishing readers the "imaginary worlds" that grant them "the freedom to position themselves in multiple ways, some of which will be recognizably 'feminine,' some 'masculine,' as we currently understand these terms, and some totally unrelated to current discursive practices" (p. 141). But, is it a facility to think that readers can simply *read their way through* "current discursive practices" and hope to achieve social and political change?

Like Trites (1997, 2000) and other feminist literary scholars (Davies, 1989; Thacker, 2001), I exerted much of my theoretical efforts on explicating the discursively constructed subject and perhaps more cautiously, the transformative promise of literature while wrestling with articulating that all-important link between individual subjectivity and social-political change. In "Faith and Hope in the Feminist Political Novel for Children: A Materialist Feminist Analysis," Angela E. Hubler (2010) presents a cogent argument that while "strong girl" novels, such as Karen Cushman's (1995) *The Midwife's Apprentice* provide girls with unconventional heroines who play to the individual, another group of books is emerging that attempts to engage YA readers on a collective political level. Turning to Meredith Cherland (1994), Hubler discusses the dangers of an over-emphasis on the individual in YA literature suggesting that these books risk attributing failure or success to qualities that are internal to individuals rather than the result of systemic oppression. In her analysis of the emphasis placed on the individual in Newbery-winning books, Cherland makes the following statement:

> Older Newbery winners like *Onion John* and *Blue Willow* serve both to *naturalize* poverty, and to assign the responsibility for the relief of such poverty to kind individuals rather than to social programs. More recent Newbery winners have treated racism as something caused by the attitude of the *individual* (Maniac McGee, for example) and poverty as the result of individual bad luck (Shiloh). Class relations, furthermore, are presented as involving the *individual's* struggle, and the *individual's* sense of responsibility, and class restrictions are often presented, in these narratives, as being overcome through an *individual's* perspicacity or an *individual's* effort.
> *(Cherland, 1994, p. 124, emphasis in the original).*

Similarly, while literacy scholars have successfully mined YA literature to promote an understanding of gender that is discursively constructed and that can be subverted by "positioned readers," we have not been so successful at demonstrating how to dismantle the actual power relations that construct difference.

It may appear that I am ready to abandon poststructuralism which recognizes the power of discourse to shape reality and its investment in the text as a self-actualizing vehicle for individual subjectivities, but reader identification has always been an invariable outgrowth of literary reading quite independent of post-structural positioning. I ask readers to consider the following from Adam Mastoon's *The Shared Heart: Portraits and Stories Celebrating Lesbian, Gay, and Bisexual Young People*:

> I read Edmund White, Bret Easton Ellis, George Whitmore, James Baldwin. I read them all for the sex . . . But while I was looking for one thing, I found another: a series of experiences, a set of emotions that echoed my own, beyond sexual desire. I found characters who were lonely like I was, sad like I was, and some characters who were happy living lives I was not even sure were possible.
>
> *(Mastoon, 1997, p. 68)*

As I have often pointed out, literature can provide both moral terrain and rich narrative possibilities that allow us to existentially explore our options for life, but in addition to my deconstructive reading of the *Kony 2012* YouTube video, other experiences in the past year have prompted me to examine more closely the insufficiency of teaching students to position themselves in autonomous opposition to essentialist gendered discourses in their reading and viewing practices with the aim of achieving social and political change.

In the course of doing historical research into the influence of teachers and teachers' unions on developing gender-equitable policy and practice in Canadian schools throughout the 1970s, I was reminded that the most significant and sustainable reforms were a collaborative grassroots effort that united educators across the country in a Marxist form of feminism focused more squarely on the material and economic (Coulter, 1996). It aimed at redressing the sexual division of labor, eradicating discriminatory practices, and equipping teachers with the knowledge and tools to understand, develop and implement gender-equitable student and staff policies. If this were not enough of a reminder that feminism had a long and productive life before poststructuralism hit the North American academy, in the same week, I received a gift from a friend—Michelle Lansberg's *Writing the Revolution* (2011). This volume chronicles the Women's Movement in Canada throughout the late 1970s and 1980s by tracing the developments in women's rights, childcare programs, educational reform, rape crisis centers, and issues related to women's work and health.

My post-poststructuralist turn was also prompted by discussions emerging from the supervision of a number of graduate theses and major research projects that focus on adolescent girls reading teen romance as a form of patriarchal resistance and in particular, one student's look back at her affinity for Francine Pascal's *Sweet Valley High* books (Malfitano, 2010). Janice Radway's (1984) *Reading the Romance* explores how such idealized narratives provide female readers a symbolic gratification—that is to say, address "basic psychological needs . . . that have been induced by the culture and its social structures but that often remain unmet in their day-to-day existence" (pp. 112–113). Radway's study of the Smithton readers, a group consisting largely of middle-class, married mothers, demonstrates how reading romance novels allowed these women to temporarily "thwart cultural expectations" (p. 211). Consistent with Radway's findings, Cherland's (1994) yearlong ethnographic study of adolescent girls' fictional reading and identity construction also demonstrated how reading romance novels might function as a form of resistance for young girls—a kind of release from patriarchal expectations and offer an escape from the "constant demands of being good" (p. 173).

The female detective novel also seems to have historically offered girls the opportunity "to protest against the available fiction of female becoming" (Miller, 1989, p. 7). Anne Lundin, in theorizing her attachment to the *Nancy Drew* detective series, has pointed to a tradition born out of gothic novels and sensational fiction of the late eighteenth and mid-nineteenth centuries written by predominantly female authors which

> aggrandized the narrative possibilities of secrets, sensational crimes, investigation, or, in the words of Jane Tompkins, 'sensational designs' . . . in the sense of presenting an alternative view of womanhood, one that idealized woman's social sphere of domesticity and revealed subversive possibilities of female agency.
>
> *(Lundin, 2003. p. 121)*

Showalter further explains:

> The sensationalists made crime and violence domestic, modern, and suburban; but their secrets were not simply solutions to mysteries and crimes; they were the secrets of women's dislike of their roles as daughters, wives, and mothers.
>
> *(Showalter, 1981, p. 158)*

While the critical work on romance reading and the sensationalists explains how my affinity for *Nancy Drew* and *Cherry Ames* escalated to my adolescent fascination with horror novels, such as *Rosemary's Baby* (Levin, 1967) and accounts of violent crimes, such as those of the Boston Strangler and Jack the Ripper, even Radway (1984) has had to conclude that despite girls and women's resistant aims, rather than take patriarchy to task, popular romance remains an active agent in sustaining the ideological status quo that continues to reconcile women and girls to patriarchal values. Nevertheless, while reading romance to escape societal demands of "being a girl" may not constitute a threat to patriarchy, many argue it is not without value. Catherine Belsey (1994) is adamant that "the great majority of stories are love stories. It seems, therefore, that people like reading about desire" (p. ix). Anne B. Thompson (2005) understands the hope expressed in Radway for a more equal world in which women and teens would no longer need this form of escape. Yet, as she recalls her love of Janet Lambert 1950s teen romance, she confides, "I counted on those happy endings to get me through adolescence, to get me right out of the daily and altogether unmelodramatic misery that I ascribed to my own life" (p. 389).

Implications for Literacy Education

While researching to write this chapter, I began to problematize the limits of my long-held assertion that young adult readers could disrupt the connection between sex and gender to defy patriarchal conventions—while I continue to believe that allowing the reader to gain an awareness of the gendered or subjected self can provide insight into patriarchal totalities. Angela Hubler (2010) argues instead for material feminist criticism as a theoretical framework that would account "for both the *ideological* and *material* realities, *subjectivity* and *politics*" (p. 63). Material feminism broadens the scope of analysis beyond the discursively constructed subject to include "representations of activism by and on behalf of girls and women" (p. 58). It emphasizes feminism's legacy in critiquing the material consequences of patriarchy while attending to the differential positioning of women. With reference to YA literature, Hubler suggests: "Fiction that reveals female oppression and offers constructions of femininity challenging traditional ones can be a powerful resource for girls seeking liberation from patriarchy" (p. 57). Phillip Serrato (2010) and Rosaura Sánchez (1996) call attention to Chicana authors, such as Sandra Cisneros, Helena Maria Viramontes, and Ana Castillo whose works of adult fiction attempt to dismantle gender hierarchies in Chicano households through a conscious rejection of patriarchal discourses and a repositioning of women within private and public spheres. Such "renarrativizations" are difficult to discern in the vast sub-genre of YA literature in which American individualism is highly prized. In contrast to the individualistic approach to female empowerment in Cushman's *The Midwife's Apprentice*, Hubler (2010) offers Trudy Krisher's (2003) *Uncommon Faith* and Joan Bauer's (2000) *Hope Was Here*, as two YA novels to engage the political on the level of both the individual and the collective. Hubler hails Krisher's *Uncommon Faith* as among the best works in children's and YA literature written about the women's rights movement in the United States. Krisher skillfully weaves in the voices of some of the most important and earliest activists in the United States to grant readers cultural and historical insight that might provide adolescent girls with more intricate ways of understanding historical contextuality, making for more culturally aware readers. These YA novels combine strong female characters with narratives of collective agency to move beyond a model of personal empowerment.

References

Advertising Research Foundation. (2011). The ARF David Ogilvy award winners and case studies. Retrieved from http://www.thearf.org/ogilvy-11-winners.php

Bauer, J. (2000). *Hope was here*. New York: G.P. Putnam's Sons.

Belsey, C. (1994). *Desire: Love stories in western culture*. Oxford: Blackwell.

Cherland, M. (1994). *Private practices: Girls reading fiction and constructing identity*. London: Taylor & Francis.

Coulter, R. (1996). Gender equity and schooling: Linking research and policy. *Canadian Journal of Education, 21,* 4, 433–452.

Cushman, K. (1995). The midwife's apprentice. New York: Clarion Books.

Davies, B. (1989). *Frogs and snails and feminist tales: Preschool children and gender*. Boston: Allen & Urwin.

Hubler, A. (2010). Faith and hope in the feminist political novel for children: A materialist feminist analysis. *The Lion and the Unicorn, 34,* 57–75.

Invisible Children. (2012). *Kony 2012*. Retrieved from http://www.youtube.com/watch?v=Y4MnpzG5Sqc

Krisher, T. (2003). *Uncommon faith*. New York: Holiday House.

Lansberg, M. (2011). *Writing the revolution*. Toronto: Second Story Press.

Levin, I. (1967). *Rosemary's baby*. New York: Pegasus Books.

Lundin, A. (2003). Every girl's good deeds: The heroics of Nancy Drew. *The Lion and the Unicorn, 27,* 1, 120–130.

Malfitano, S. (2010). *The function of adolescent romance: An analysis of Sweet Valley High* (unpublished masters thesis). Toronto: York University.

Mastoon, A. (1997). *The shared heart: Portraits and stories celebrating lesbian, gay, and bisexual young people*. New York: HarperCollins.

Miller, N. (1989). *Subject to change: Reading feminist writing*. New York: Columbia University Press.

Radway, J. (1984). *Reading the romance: Women, patriarchy, and popular literature*. Chapel Hill, NC: University of North Carolina Press.

Sánchez, R. (1996). Deconstruction and renarrativizations: Trends in Chicana literature. *Bilingual Review/Revista bilingüe, 21,* 1, 52–58.

Serrato, P. (2010). Promise and peril: The gendered implications of Pat Mora's *Pablo's tree* and Ana Castillo's *My daughter, my son, the eagle, the dove. Children's Literature, 38,* 133–152.

Showalter, E. (1977). *A literature of their own: British women novelists from Brontë to Lessing*. Princeton, NJ: Princeton University Press.

Showalter, E. (1981). Feminist criticism in the wilderness. *Critical Inquiry, 8,* 189–206.

Swifferbreakup. (Nov. 30, 2007). Swiffer "courtroom" commercial. Retrieved from http://www.youtube.com/watch?v=dZYt5L56gss&feature=relmfu

Swifferbreakup. (Nov. 30, 2007). Swiffer "debate" commercial. Retrieved from http://www.youtube.com/watch?v=M24TR6ULIb0&feature=relmfu

Taylor, M. (1981). *Let the circle be unbroken*. New York: Puffin.

Thacker, D. (2001). Feminine language and the politics of children's literature. *The Lion and the Unicorn, 25,* 3–16.

Thompson, A. (2005). Rereading fifties teen romance: Reflections on Janet Lambert. *The Lion and the Unicorn, 29,* 373–396.

Trites, R. (1997). *Waking Sleeping Beauty: Feminist voices in children's novels*. Iowa City: University of Iowa Press.

Trites, R. (2000). *Disturbing the universe: Power and repression in adolescent literature*. Iowa City: University of Iowa Press.

3

MASCULINITY AND PORTRAYALS OF AFRICAN AMERICAN BOYS IN YOUNG ADULT LITERATURE

A Critical Deconstruction and Reconstruction of this Genre

Thomas W. Bean and Theodore Ransaw

> "I sit in your class, I play by the rules. I'm young, I'm fly, I'm black. So of course I think I'm cool."
>
> *(Flake, 2010, p .3).*

Young adult literature is often regarded as a powerful genre that engages adolescents in extended periods of reading with the potential to contribute to students' reading achievement (Bean et al., 2013; Guthrie & McRae, 2011). Within the sub-genre of young adult literature featuring African American boy characters, award-winning books by Walter Dean Myers and Sharon Flake stand out. For example, *Monster* (Myers, 2001) chronicles the incarceration of 16-year-old Steve Harmon following a convenience store robbery and murder. Filled with postmodern features including font shifts and scenes that include Steve's diary entries, court transcripts and other text forms, this novel portrays African American youth in a particular fashion that lends itself to critique. Groenke and Youngquist note that, "Steve—besieged by competing discourses about black male youth—never locates a coherent self." Indeed, these authors argue that:

> Steve struggles throughout the book to understand who he is as an African American male, a star student, and a loving son and brother in a society that tells him he can be only one of two things: a thug or sellout.
>
> *(Groenke & Youngquist, 2011, p. 506)*

In the world of the lockup where Steve finds himself following his role as a lookout in the convenience store robbery, being masculine means being tough, fighting, and showing no fear. As we examine this sub-genre, a trend depicting

African American males as criminalized and besieged with problems emerges. In the sections that follow we briefly describe masculine theory and its role in countering and critiquing taken-for-granted stereotypes. In addition, we examine current thinking about masculine theory in light of African American boys and the art of "cool." We then apply this theory to a critical literacy examination of Sharon Flakes' (2010) young adult collection, *You Don't Even Know Me*. And finally we offer counterpoint young adult literature titles that depict male African American youth in a different light, outside prison walls and street life. We also offer some response strategies that you can use when engaging your students in close reading of young adult literature about African American youth.

Masculine Theory

Masculine theory posits that masculinity is an identity performance or social construction, amenable to critique and change (Bean & Harper, 2007). Rigidly narrow views of what it means to be masculine predispose boys to act in ways that reify male power. For those youth who do not or cannot enact gender and sexual norms within a narrow, hegemonic model of what it means to be male, the consequences are often devastating. Name-calling, bullying, assault and suicide loom as distinct possibilities when the worst forms of hegemonic masculinity are in play in middle and high school settings. Scholars associated with masculine theory note that hegemonic masculinity is largely centered around opposition to feminine roles (Weaver-Hightower, 2003). Power accrues to jocks and other masculine figures in middle and secondary school settings.

That said, schools can be sites of inquiry and critique into forms of social difference, including gender. Bean and Harper (2007) noted that: "Masculine theory, like feminist theory, opens up the possibility of examining how gender is scripted in text and in life, with the hope of transforming social scripts and their enactments" (p. 13). While this view is optimistic, critiquing and transforming well-established gender roles is by no means easy. Examining gender and literacy from an interactive perspective suggest that school-based literacy practices position males in passive and potentially quiet roles that clash with entrenched male values.

Gender and Literacy

There are at least two contrasting perspectives regarding gender and literacy. One perspective is that schooling is patriarchal, restrictive, and limiting to women and their efforts to function as full participants in a male-dominated working world. For example, Weaver-Hightower (2003) notes that masculinity is a defining element in education and that male-dominant gender and gender roles are tied to the smooth functioning of society and consequently influence schooling. Curriculum textbooks especially locate women as limited while men are shown as leaders (Weaver-Hightower 2003).

The other perspective is that because of the overwhelming amount of White middle-class female teachers in American schools, education has become feminized for boys. Many teenage boys are turned off to reading because it is considered for "nerds" and is uncool (Brozo, 2005), and outside the construction of masculinity (Archer & Yamashita, 2003). In fact, there has been concern about the feminine and frilly content of elementary education since the late 1960s (Connell, 1996). Boys are at a disadvantage by feminized forms of teaching more likely to reward quiet sitting and non-competitive behavior (Martino, 2008). Studies show that girls outperform boys in almost every related category of reading (OECD, 2006), a contributing factor to the low percentage of male high school graduation.

While these two perspectives seem disparate, in fact they both share a common vantage point from the standpoint of hegemonic masculinity. In other words, hegemonic masculinity is central to many of the struggles boys face in literacy (Martino & Kehler, 2007) across both perspectives. Both girls as well as African American boys are the subordinated groups. In 2003, 2005, 2007, and 2009, Black boys scored the lowest in reading proficiency in 4th grade, and in 2009 Black males scored 42% lower than White males at meeting college reading level benchmarks (Lewis, et al., 2010).

But we want to expand on these two perspectives by adding an often over-looked sociological issue when considering African American boys and reading engagement and performance. Research on African male masculinity expands our thinking about reading and what it means to be male and "cool."

Reading and the Art of Cool

Reading is typically a quiet, contemplative activity. Photos of teens sitting and reading generally depict this process as solitary and silent versus active and exciting. As a result, boys often reject reading, considering it for *nerds* and *uncool* (Brozo, 2005), well outside the construction of masculinity (Archer & Yamashita, 2003). But what is cool? Everyone knows what cool is *not*, but how do we define what *is* cool?

Reading a book has been described as acting White [read uncool] for Black boys (Buck, 2010). However, it is not simply the act of reading that is uncool. Any action that is not appropriate based on White norms of hegemonic masculinity for the minoritized is viewed as uncool. In fact, elite nineteenth-century English masculinity was associated with natural mental superiority (Cohen, 1998). It is the social advantages of the upper class White male that lead to the impression that success should appear effortless. After all, privileged men do not work hard. This holds true in life and in the classroom as well. Reay (2004) asserts the "effortless generation of scholarship" is part of the idealized norm. "For those who have prior advantage application becomes pedantry and a respect for hard work grinding, limited pettiness" (Bourdieu & Passeron, 1979, p. 24, cited in Reay, 2004, p. 36). This "it is uncool to work" discourse has become a norm among middle-class and working-class boys and is not restricted to "race" or ethnic group (Francis & Archer, 2005). In fact, this "uncool to work hard in school" phenomenon is the topic of several research articles (Francis, 1999; Frosh et al., 2002; Archer & Yamashita, 2003; Younger & Warrington, 2005; Jackson & Dempster, 2009; Francis et al., 2009). It has even been argued that, to be a boy is to "succeed without trying" (Hodgetts, 2008, p. 476) and that academic hard work is often incompatible with "cool" masculinities in many schools (Frosh et al., 2002; Younger & Warrington, 2005; Jackson & Dempster, 2009). However, even the walk or stroll—the tendency of African American males to swagger—has forced teachers to consider Black boys more likely to attain lower academic achievement, to be in need of special education services and to act aggressively (Neal, 2003).

In other words, in an effort to avoid being perceived as uncool, many boys who are successful in school sometimes try to make it look effortless (Jackson & Dempster, 2009). These academically successful boys are attempting to balance their social capital with their academic capital. Bourdieu (1986) defines social capital as networks and connections that can be transmitted to children. The concepts of social capital are ways in which social bonds of shared values such as trust add value to individuals and organizations (McGrath & Van Buskirk, 1996). Social capital is intrinsically related to academic capital since schools are communal organizations (McGrath & Van Buskirk, 1996). Sullivan and Sheffrin (2003) describe academic capital as related to human capital [potential], measured by knowledge and skills reflected by education or, as Bourdieu (1986) described it, the social transmission of schooling through family and culture. This balancing act, between being social and being a scholar, is an attempt to find a "middle way" between schoolwork and "cool work" (Frosh et al., 2002, p. 205). The avoidance of being perceived as socially inept is more than just a form of social capital; it is also a matter of survival to not be bullied (Frosh et al., 2002).

Gender, Sexuality, and the Art of Cool

Effort and diligence are associated with femininity, and femininity remains masculinity's subordinated other (Dweck, 2000). Weaver-Hightower (2003) reminds us that not only is cool determined by race, ethnicity and class, but by accepted norms of sexuality as well. Even the educational success of girls and women has not broken the stigma that working hard in school is for girls (Hodgetts, 2008). So in essence, the effortless demonstration of masculinity also known as being cool can be viewed as a cultural archetype (Jung et al., 1964) significantly intersecting class with race, sexuality, gender and nationality (Connell, 2002) and related to ideology, and interpersonal relationships in adolescent ethnic identity (Steinberg, 1993; McKenry et al., 1989). Cool is more than not acting White, it is the performance of masculinity based on looking relaxed and effortless in challenging tasks including reading.

The Praxis of Cool

The art of effortless cool serves a twofold purpose. One, not working hard and looking cool is rewarded by others and affirms masculinity by avoiding femininity and, two, failure can be attributed to a lack of effort, not the lack of ability and any success can be attributed to effortless natural ability (Hodgetts, 2008; Dweck, 2000; Cohen, 1998; Covington, 1998). This stands in stark contrast to other perspectives of Black masculinity that merely focus on Black boys who are forced to choose between being popular or smart (Kunjufu, 1988), a thug or sellout (Groenke & Youngquist, 2011), or the frequently misinterpreted views of Ogbu, that Black boys suffer from the oppositional culture and therefore are afraid to act White (Ogbu, 2004). This work has been misinterpreted because Ogbu actually asserted that both societal and school discrimination, along with instrumental community factors such as perceptions about the lack of jobs and Black oppositional culture are three interrelated factors in which to examine Black student low academic behavior.

Often described as a *cool pose* (Majors & Billson, 1992) or a withdrawal from study and immersion into sports, it offers African American boys the appearance of being resilient, relaxed, confident, and emotionally detached (Hecht et al., 2003). These perspectives serve to reinforce the idea that resistance to education is a rite of passage for Black boys who are trying to enact coolness.

However, we believe that the lack of engagement in reading for Black boys is more nuanced than just the binary opposition of the smart boys or academic achievers, and the cool boys, commonly known as the athletes or jocks (Connell, 1996). We assert that different communities read texts in complex and different ways (Heath, 1983) and that Black boys need to be understood within the relational context of their experience in America (Hillard, 1995), as well being perceived as individuals with the ability to self-regulate reading engagement (Guthrie & McRae, 2011). Indeed, a growing body of young adult literature offers teachers and African American male teens a more complex and nuanced vision of how to overcome the hegemonic elements of masculinity described thus far in this chapter.

Implications for Teaching with Young Adult Literature

"Literacy education has to have a strong gravitational pull for African American male adolescents [that speaks] in their present-day contexts" (Tatum, 2008, p. 163) in order to effectively break these gendered and cultural norms. For example, it *is* possible to engage Black boys in reading by utilizing multifaceted texts such as Sharon Flakes' *You Don't Even Know Me* (2010) that explore complex identities of Black male masculinity.

Flake allows the reader to explore multiple points of view by incorporating short stories and poems that engage different narratives. The following selection is an example of how peer pressure and pride, social pressure and self-efficacy are constantly at odds for young males.

> Willie would say I'm a wuss, a punk or something worse, but I move even closer and kiss my dad on the side of his neck. I am not embarrassed. This is my father. I'm his son.
>
> *(Flake, 2010, p. 80)*

This method of multi-genre writing highlights the "power and privilege within masculinities, and recognize that masculinities are complicated and multifaceted and may even be contradictory" (Wedgwood, 2009, p. 336). Put another way, hegemonic masculinity is a practice that is constantly being recreated under changing conditions, including resistance by subordinate groups (Wedgwood, 2009), and not a fixed biological behavior (Bean & Harper, 2007).

We advocate for more culturally and gender-enabling texts such as *Monster* and *You Don't Even Know Me* that move beyond "unrealistic evaluations of deficiency towards any other group that is not White or middle class based on White males as the control group" (Padilla, 2004, p. 129). Tatum defines an *enabling text* as, "one that moves beyond a solely cognitive focus—such as skill and strategy development—to include a social, cultural, political, spiritual, or economic focus" (2008, 164). This idea is supported by research that insists culturally responsive management practices can work with White teachers and African American students (Brown, 2003) and reduce problems associated with discipline. All teachers can get Black boys to respond if they incorporate culturally competent practices such as using music [hip-hop], introducing hobbies [sports] and artifacts and implementing relevant storytelling teaching strategies (Shade et al., 2004). What is needed in culturally responsive teaching with multicultural young adult literature is understanding the needs and experiences of students' cultural knowledge, acknowledging their prior experiences, accepting their frames of reference and affirming their cultural learning styles to make learning relevant and effective (Gay, 2000).

A growing body of young adult literature offers educators complex literary terrain to engage African American males in critical literacy practices that interrogate what it means to be male and a reader. These titles include:

> *Bad boy: A Memoir*, by Walter Dean Myers. A prolific writer who was teased as a child because he stuttered, recounts his life as a child. This book situates the author as first person who expresses handling the peer pressure that stems from looking too studious by putting the books he took home from the library in brown paper bags.

> Betsey Franco's book *Do You Hear Me?*, is a multi-genre book written by teenage boys for teenage boys from a multitude of perspectives. Topics include religion and sex and it uses strong language. What's not to love?

Sharon Flake's *No Boys Allowed!* For young readers about the frustration a boy feels when he is restricted from jumping rope because it's supposedly a sport just for girls.

References

Archer, L. & Yamashita, H. (2003). Theorizing Inner-city Masculinities: "race," class, gender and education. *Gender & Education, 15*(2), 115.

Bean, T.W. & Harper, H. (2007). Reading men differently: Alternative portrayals of masculinity in contemporary young adult fiction. *Reading Psychology, 28*(1), 11–30.

Bean, T.W., Dunkerly, J., & Harper, H. (2013). *Teaching young adult literature: Developing students as world citizens.* Thousand Oaks, CA: Sage.

Bourdieu, P. (1986). The forms of capital. In John, G. Richardson (Ed.), *Handbook of theory and research for the sociology of education.* New York: Greenwood Press.

Brown, D.F. (2003). Urban teachers' use of culturally responsive management strategies. *Theory Into Practice, 42*(4), 277–282.

Brozo, D.F. (2012). *Outside Interest and Literate Practices as Contexts for Increasing Engagement and Critical Reading for Adolescent Boys.* In B. Guzzetti & Tom Bean's (Eds.). *Adolescent literacies and the gendered self: (Re) constructing identities through multimodal literacy practices.* New York: Routledge.

Brozo, W.G. (2005). Gender and reading literacy. *Reading Today, 22*(4), 18.

Buck, W. (2010). *Acting white: The ironic legacy of desegregation.* New Haven, CT: Yale University Press.

Cohen, M., (1998). "A habit of healthy idleness": Boys' underachievement in historical perspective. In: D. Epstein et al., (Eds.) *Failing boys? Issues in gender and achievement.* Buckingham: Open University Press, 19–34.

Connell, R.W. (1996). Teaching boys: New research on masculinity, and gender strategies for schools. *Teachers College Record, 98*(2), 206–235.

Connell, R.W. (2002). *Gender.* Cambridge: Polity Press/Malden: Blackwell Publishers.

Connell, R.W. (2005). *Masculinities,* 2nd ed. Cambridge: Polity Press.

Covington, M.V. (1998). *The will to learn: A guide for motivating young people. Cambridge*: Cambridge University Press.

Dweck, C.S., 2000. *Self-theories: Their role in motivation, personality and development.* Hove: Taylor & Francis.

Flake, S.G. (2004). No boys allowed! New York: Zenderkidz.

Flake, S.G. (2005). *Bang.* New York: Hyperion/Jump at the Sun.

Flake, S.G. (2010). *You don't even know me: Stories and poems about boys.* New York: Hyperion/Jump at the Sun.

Francis, B. (1999) Lads, lasses and (New) Labour: 14–16 year old students' responses to the laddish behavior of boys and boys' underachievement debate. *British Journal of Sociology of Education, 20,* 355–371.

Francis, B. & Archer, L. (2005). Negotiating the dichotomy of Boffin and Triad: British-Chinese pupils' constructions of 'laddism'. *Sociological review, 53*(3), 495–521.

Francis, B., Skelton, C., & Read, B. (2009). The simultaneous production of educational achievement and popularity: How do some pupils accomplish it? *British Educational Research Journal, 36*(2): 317–340.

Franco, B. (Ed.). (2001). *Do you hear me? Poems and writings by teenage boys.* Somerville, MA: Candlewick Press.

Frosh, S., Phoenix, A., & Pattman, R. (2002). *Young masculinities: Understanding boys in contemporary society*. Basingstoke: Palgrave.

Gay, G. (2000). *Culturally responsive teaching: Theory, research, and practice*. New York: Teachers College Press.

Groenke, S.L. & Youngquist, M. (2011). "Are we postmodern yet?" Reading *Monster* with 21st century ninth graders. *Journal of Adolescent & Adult Literacy, 54*(7), 505–513.

Guthrie, J.T. & McRae, A. (2011). Reading engagement among African American and European-American students. In S.J. Samuels & A.E. Farstrup (Eds.), *What research has to say about reading instruction* (4th ed.), (pp. 115–142). Newark, DE: International Reading Association.

Heath, S.B. (1983). *Ways with words: Language, life and the work in communities and classrooms*. Mahwah, NJ: Lawrence Erlbaum.

Hecht, M.L., Jackson, R.L., & Ribeau, S.A. (2003). *African American communication: Exploring identity and culture (2nd edition)*. Mahwah, New Jersey: Lawrence Erlbaum Associates.

Hillard, A. (1995). *The maroon within us: Selected essays on African American community socializations*. Baltimore, MD: Black Classic Press.

Hodgetts, K., (2008). Underperformance or "getting it right"? Constructions of gender and achievement in the Australian inquiry into boys' education. *British Journal of Sociology of Education, 29*(5), 465–477.

Jackson, C. & Dempster, S. (2009). "I sat back on my computer . . . with a bottle of whisky next to me": constructing "cool" masculinity through "effortless" achievement in secondary and higher education. *Journal of Gender Studies, 18*(4), December, 341–356.

Jung, C.G., von Franz, M.L., Henderson, J.L., Jacobi, J. Jaffe, A., & Freeman, J. (Eds.), (1964). *Man and his symbols*. New York: Anchor Books Doubleday.

Kunjufu, J. (1988). *To be popular or smart: The Black peer group*. Chicago: African American Images.

Lewis, S., Simon, C., Uzzell, R., Horwtiz, A., & Casserly, M. (2010). *A Call for change: The social and educational factors contributing to the outcomes of Black males in urban schools*. Washington, DC: The Council of Great City Schools.

Majors, R. & Billson, J.M. (1992). *Cool pose: The dilemmas of Black manhood in America*. New York: Lexington Books.

Martino, W. (2008). The lure of hegemonic masculinity: Investigating the dynamics of gender relations in male elementary school teachers' lives. *International Journal of Qualitative Studies in Education 21*(6), 575–603.

Martino, W. & Berrill, D. (2003). Boys, schooling and masculinities: Interrogating the "right" way to educate boys. *Educational Review, 55*(2), 99–117.

Martino, W. & M.D. Kehler, (2007). Gender-based literacy reform: A question of challenging or recuperating gender binaries. Special Issue "Boys, Literacy and Schooling", Guest Editors: M. Kehler & W. Martino, *Canadian Journal of Education 30*(2), pp. 406–431.

McGrath, D. & Van Buskirk, B. (1996). Social and emotional capital in education: Cultures of support for at risk students. *Journal of Developmental Education 1*(1).

McKenry, P., Everett, J., Ramseur, H., & Carter, C. (1989). Research on Black adolescents: A legacy of cultural bias. *Journal of Adolescent Research, 4*, 254–64.

Myers, W.D. (2001). *Bad boy: A memoir*. New York: HarperCollins.

Myers, W.D. (2001). *Monster*. New York: Amistad.

Neal, L. (2003). The effects of African American movement styles on teachers' perceptions and reactions. *Journal of Special Education, 37*(2), 98–120.

OECD, Office of Economic Co-operation and Development. (2006). Education at a glance. Retrieved, January 3, at www.oecd.eog. ISBN 9264025316.

Ogbu, J. (2004). *Minority status, oppositional culture, & schooling: Sociocultural, political, and historical studies in education.* New York: Routledge.

Padilla A.M. (2004). Quantitative methods in multicultural education research. In J. Banks & C. Banks (Eds.), *Handbook of Research in Multicultural Education* (second ed.). San Francisco: Jossey-Bass.

Reay, D. (2004). Cultural capitalists and academic habitus: Classed and gendered labour in UK higher education. *Women's Studies International Forum*, 27(1), 31–39.

Shade, B.J. Kelly, C., & Oberg, M. (2004). *Creating culturally responsive classrooms.* Washington, DC: American Psychological Association.

Steinberg, L. (1993). *Adolescence* (3rd ed.), New York: McGraw-Hill.

Sullivan A. & Steven M. Sheffrin (2003). *Economics: Principals in action.* Upper Saddle River, NJ: Pearson Prentice Hall.

Tatum, A.W. (2008). Toward a more anatomically complete model of literacy instruction: A focus on African male adolescents and texts. *Harvard Educational Review*, 78(1), 155–180.

Tayor-Butler, C. (2003). *No boys allowed!* New York: Scholastic Printing.

Weaver-Hightower, M. (2003). The "boy turn" in research on gender and education. *Review of Educational Research*, 73(4), 471–498.

Wedgwood, N. (2009). Connell's theory of masculinity—its origins and influences on the study of Gender. *Journal of Gender Studies* 18(4), 329–339.

Younger, M. & Warrington, M. (2005). *Raising boys' achievement in secondary schools.* Maidenhead: Open University Press.

4

ONE WORLD

Understanding the Discourse of Benevolent Girlhood through Critical Media Literacy

Elizabeth Marshall and Özlem Sensoy

Tweens, a subset of the teen generation, are those girls "in between" childhood and teens. Typically identified as between 8 and 14 years, this group is a key global demographic for marketers. Tweens' annual disposable income is estimated anywhere between 1.5 and 10 billion dollars (Castleberry & Merrier, 2008; Prince & Martin, 2011). They are also brand and celebrity conscious, influence family buying patterns to the tune of 260 billion dollars a year, own mobile devices and access media at unprecedented rates (Castleberry & Merrier, 2008; Prince & Martin, 2011). For these reasons, marketers and corporations seek access to this lucrative demographic through a variety of popular cultural texts including books, magazines, films, music, and video games.

Not an official curriculum, these cultural texts are often dismissed as "just entertainment" by parents and educators. However, media liter\acy scholars have researched the relationship between youth and popular culture for some time. This research is broadly organized around: examining the ideological messages within pop culture and media texts (Kellner & Share, 2007; Jiwani, 2006; Staples, 2008); exploring marketing and corporate activities surrounding kids' texts (e.g., Campaign for a Commercial Free Childhood; Marshall & Sensoy, 2011); and, examining transgressive uses of media by youth, such as fanzines, fansubbing, or video blogging (Kearney, 2006; Jenkins, 2006). Taken together, this scholarship invites educators to consider how popular cultural texts, and the multiple literacies that they require, factor into the lives of youth as a form of "cultural pedagogy" (Steinberg & Kincheloe, 2004).

Contemporary popular cultural texts often have a global reach as these texts travel across national borders through a range of media. In addition, popular cultural narratives often present storylines aimed at creating or representing youth as global citizens. In this chapter, we focus on the cultural pedagogy of Disney's mega girl-franchise "The Cheetah Girls" and the construction of the "global girl citizen" (Burns, 2008) within these materials. Our conceptual analysis centers on the franchise's last film *One World*. We examine the role of marketing and corporate activities related to the tween girl market that the Cheetah Girls products target, as well as examine the ideologies about girlhood—especially the relational politics among "different" global girls—that shape the bulk of the Cheetah Girls materials.

Popular Culture, Media, and Critical Media Literacy

In our own experiences in classrooms and as teacher educators, we see the prevalence of media and pop culture in our students' lives, illustrating how important it is to help students critically examine and re-imagine popular culture and media in relationship to education. We work to complicate the idea that popular culture is either bad or good, and instead, invite students to look at familiar movies, books, games, etc. as spaces where meanings are created as well as contested, complicating the idea that audiences (especially youth) are naive, passive, or disengaged. There are two important ideas that need definition before proceeding to critical media literacy: *popular culture*, and *media*.

Popular culture is a challenging term to define, especially given that the stuff of popular culture becomes dated almost as quickly as it is produced. Drawing on John Storey's (2009) work, popular culture:

- Describes texts like Michael Jackson's *Thriller* album that are or were widely liked by many people;
- Refers to things that are less sophisticated or considered "low" culture;
- Reflects a consumer culture that is produced for mass consumption (e.g. McDonald's Happy Meal toys);
- Provides a place for creating new forms of expression as well as a vehicle for critique through tactics such as culture jamming (the rewriting of media, such as corporate logos or advertisements in a way that subverts or overturns taken-for-granted meanings).

Media (tools/technologies of communication) of previous generations may have referred to newspapers, magazines, and books. Today's media, however, include an explosion of online/global networking systems (Twitter, Facebook, Bebo, Reddit, Tumblr, YouTube, Pinterest) as well as a music and film culture that has grown to a sophisticated machinery of marketing and selling of culture, lifestyle, and products via videos, product placements, and synchronized releases. Cross-marketing between and among corporately structured partners has become the norm (Marshall & Sensoy, 2011).

Media literacy, an approach to understanding the relationship between popular culture and media, refers to the skills involved in decoding, analyzing, and using media-based popular cultural texts (print, electronic, and digital). Douglas Kellner and Jeff Share (2007) offered useful distinctions between media literacy and *critical media literacy*. Media literacy approaches sometimes focus solely on arts-based or technology literacy development (for instance, learning how to use software to create multimedia presentations or creative editing of images); and/or it can sometimes take a "protectionist approach" that seeks to limit kids' viewing of certain media texts as a way to protect them from "bad" media. In contrast, a *critical media literacy* approach builds on and strengthens these strategies by developing the ability to analyze media as a space where power is created as well as contested. As Kellner and Share write:

> There is expanding recognition that media representations help construct our images and understanding of the world and that education must meet the dual challenges of teaching media literacy in a multicultural society and sensitizing students and the public to inequities and injustices of a society based on gender, race, and class inequalities and discrimination.
>
> *(Kellner & Share, 2005, p. 370)*

This approach fosters examination of ideological messages coded into texts, analyzes the production and circulation of media and the corporate activities surrounding popular culture texts, and also recognizes that audiences are not passive but rather active and capable critics and revisers of media culture.

The Cheetah Girls: A Corporate Invention

The Cheetah Girls are a Disney-created girl group based on a book series about a multiracial group of girl friends played by Kiely Williams (as fashionista Aquanetta), Sabrina Bryan (as the foster child dancer Dorinda), Raven Symone (as the group's leader Galleria), and Adrienne Bailon (as the heart of the group, Chanel). The girls attend a New York high school and have ambitions to be superstars. They are best friends who love to sing, dance, design their own costumes, and shop. The Cheetah Girls first appeared in a 16-book series of bestselling books written by Deborah Gregory and published by Disney in the late 1990s. Disney approached Gregory to create a series about a girl singing group. At the time, Gregory was working as a columnist for *Essence* magazine.

The fictional lives of the Cheetah Girls played out in the three movies, music CDs, video games, and books about their lives and friendship. Along with the fictional lives, the Cheetah Girls were a live musical act. While the group, which was created in 2003 officially disbanded in 2008, the girls have since worked on solo projects, and were the precursors to other Disney-produced acts, such as the *High School Musical* series, the Jonas Brothers, Hannah Montana/Miley Cyrus, Demi Lovato, Selena Gomez, and many other tween stars—many of whom toured with the Cheetah Girls.

In 2003, the soundtrack to their first, self-titled Disney channel film reached double platinum (over two million copies sold) and according to Nielsen SoundScan, rivalled the sales of pop stars Beyoncé, Outkast, and Coldplay that year(http://findarticles.com/p/articles/mi_m0EIN/is_2003_Dec_31/ai_1117765 84/). According to music industry figures published in *Billboard* magazine, by the end of 2003, *The Cheetah Girls* soundtrack was outperforming soundtracks from popular films, including *Chicago, The Lion King, Shrek,* and *Pirates of the Caribbean* (Billboard, 2003). While their Disney site is still live, the Cheetah Girls disbanded in 2008; however their success, popularity, and status as an exemplar of the Disney-machinery-created pop culture for tweens, makes them a productive example for analysis.

Ideologies and Corporate Activities in the Cheetah Girls

The most common critiques of popular cultural texts aimed at girls tend to focus on the sexualization of girls' bodies and/or the empowerment (or lack of empowerment) of girl characters within such narratives. For instance, the Cheetah Girls were consistently associated with innocence and described in the mainstream media as "bubble gum pop" and "as the Spice Girls minus spice but plus Splenda" (Heffernan, 2006). Furthermore, as Sharon Lamb and Lyn Mikel Brown (2006) pointed out, "The Cheetah Girls are more interesting than girl pop stars who don't play instruments and just stand there and sing" (p. 143). It's true that the Cheetah Girls *do* offer representations of friendship across racial and class differences. Two of the Cheetah Girls are African American, one is Latina, and the fourth is White, but grew up in low-income foster care (unlike the other three affluent girls). In addition, the girls represent not only racial diversity, but also body diversity that is rare in mainstream representations for girls. For these reasons, the series makes important headway in unsettling normative ideas about girlhood.

These diverse and empowering representations make it easy to forget that the Cheetah Girls are a mega-franchise. The machinery of the Cheetah Girls brand churns beneath the surface of girlhood innocence. In addition to the predictable products that might be associated with a Disney group—such as books, dolls, CDs, DVDs, sing-a-long CDs, concert tours—there are also household goods, such as bed sheets, toothbrushes, various Cheetah Girls-themed games on Game Boy and Nintendo systems, as well as online virtual games. Not surprisingly, the games focus on dancing and fashion. For example, in the Nintendo game, *Cheetah Girls: Passport to Stardom*, players travel with the Cheetah Girls in international dance competitions where, according to the game, "Players can also customize hundreds of outfits, choosing from an array of Indian-inspired fashions, as well as classic Cheetah Girls styles." The Cheetah Girls "sing, dance, and accessorize their way around the world." Players compete in a series of "dance-offs" from the Cheetah Girls movies and play mini-games to perfect fashions from international cities—New York, Barcelona, and Mumbai (the locations of the three Cheetah Girls films). As the Cheetah Girls dance their way around the world, players are invited to join an online community of Disney gamers—creating 3D avatars, profiles, and engaging in chat with other fans in chat rooms. Participation in these forums gives players in-game honors and unlocks exclusive Disney content.

History of the Global Girl

While it would be easy to bemoan the Cheetah Girls as a contemporary example of the ills of corporate culture, the script that makes this group so successful is recycled from previous youth brands. That is, the Cheetah Girls are part of a long history of popular cultural texts aimed at adolescent girl consumers in which the trope of travel allows girls to imagine themselves as the "global girl-citizen" (Burns, 2008). For instance, in the early 1900s, American publishers of mass-market books for teens produced stories about traveling adolescent girlfriends in series like the *Motor Maids* (1913) and in the Nancy Drew mysteries in which the famous teen girl sleuth travels to China, Japan, and Turkey to solve cases (Marshall, 2012). Disney's Cheetah Girls product, then, follows a familiar and successful script that relies on imaginary representations of other places and people. In this script, the North American girl's empowerment is represented through friendships with girls from a range of non-North American, non-European locations. Difference between and among girls from different global locations is constructed as positive, and girls' presumed shared interests in clothes, food, and music exceed any racial, religious, and/or class disparities that might create and sustain hierarchical relationships. Thus, when girl power goes "Cheetah-licious" it relies on a commodification of global differences in which superficial aspects of culture (such as dress and dance) are presented as uniting girls around the world in a solidarity of sisterhood.

With transnational travel and the inclusion of global girls (specifically in their second and third films set in Spain and India), the Cheetah Girls materials construct an understanding of girl friendships as a universal, globally-organized condition about benevolence, goodness, and whiteness. In particular, travel allows the Cheetah Girls a "global" experience. For example, in *One World* the girls fly from New York to India and, through the fictional representation of contact with "Other" girls, the film provides North American audiences and particularly tween girls an education. The film offers lessons in "girl empowerment" (or more accurately, Western, American girls empowering their less-fortunate "global" girl sisters) that make the very real differences among girls invisible.

The Cheetah Girls flattens differences between girls, and offers tween consumers a range of de-politicized, racialized girlhoods to learn about and consume. From the multiracial make up of the Cheetah Girls to the global girlfriends they meet outside of the United States (in Spain, they dance in the streets, sit at sidewalk cafes marveling at the architecture, and learn to dance the tango as part of a heterosexual love story), these global girls are cosmopolitan subjects who travel and are knowledgeable about the world. Kellie Burns (2008) wrote that, "The project of constructing global girl-citizens both in schools and beyond is also invested in helping girls imagine themselves as cosmopolitan citizens with access to a broader range of 'cultural' experiences" (p. 353). In each of the examples above, the idea of *benevolence* is central; North American girls are constructed as girls who understand and help *other* girls across national borders.

In this way, the series relies on the "commodification of race and gender difference" (duCille, 1994, p. 48) to market the Cheetah Girl texts and related products as multicultural. In the final Cheetah Girls film, *One World*, the girls travel to India to appear in a Bollywood movie. Once there, they realize that only one of them can be the star. The promotional materials for the film read, "They've rocked the U.S., taken Spain by storm, and now they're off to India for an adventure of a lifetime." Imaginary travel to Other countries allows girls in the "West" to make visits to girls in other locales as the promotional blurb invites viewers to consume the differences made available throughout the Disney corporation's construction of the Other. As one of the "real" Cheetah Girls, Adrienne Bailon told an interviewer about the *One World* movie: "Kids are really going to see what a vibrant culture India has. They are going to love the clothing, the dancing, the music. It's super-festive." Here, transnational travel is sold to consumers as an authentic experience whereby viewers come to experience and "know" another culture via a superficial multiculturalism. As Bailon's words suggest, the primary differences to engage with when traveling the world are easy to identify and festive—food, clothes, and different styles of music and dance. Difference, then, is about a knowable and consumable cultural other defined in relationship to the needs and desires of a presumed Western tween girl audience. Global girlhood products are available for immediate consumption, and the Cheetah Girls products suggest that the world is "small and cultural difference is consumable" (duCille, 1994, p. 49). Thus, diversity is not so much a condition, but a strategy to sell that marketers have been using since at least the late 1960s (duCille, 1994).

Travel signifies "a universal form of mobility" (Grewal, 1996, p. 2). The Cheetah Girls move without constraints and cross borders without difficulty. Neither immigrants nor displaced persons, The Cheetah Girls hold U.S. passports that allow them to travel freely, especially because their travel is defined in terms of adventure and benevolence. The Cheetah Girls are part of a larger girlhood curriculum in which the contemporary global girl-citizen can consume and imagine the world through film, computer games, books and other products created for and marketed to the contemporary girl.

The Cheetah Girls are one example of a larger pedagogy aimed at schooling North American girls in how to be good and get along across differences. The Cheetah Girls even offer readers a list of "rules" whereby bridges among global girls can be built. A girl should be nice, think about others before herself, try not to complain, have a signature fashion style, adopt a heterosexual lifestyle, dream of an unrealistic career, such as becoming a music or movie star, work hard, and listen to her parents. The Cheetah Girls series relies on marketing strategies of contemporary globalization that have co-opted global diversities into a marketplace of multiculturalism aimed at selling the idea of the global girl-citizen as the empowered American girl who finds her cosmopolitanism by consuming the right products.

The representation of girlhood here relies on the idea of "doing good" in other places as a form of regulation that positions girls back into traditional helping roles. In our other work (Sensoy & Marshall, 2010) we have named this type of girlhood help "missionary girl power." Missionary girl power refers to the discursive strategies that construct "First World" girls of the global north as the saviors or the benevolent helpers of their "Third World" sisters. In *One World*, the Cheetah Girls give up their own dreams of fame in order to help the choreographer, Gita, find her true calling and her true love. If it hadn't been for the help of the Cheetah Girls, Gita would have spent her life unhappily living out her constrained existence. Benevolence—the desire to help others—and the re-assertion of an imaginary binary between the West and other locations runs across all the platforms of the Cheetah Girl brand, including interviews with the real Cheetah Girl stars. For example, as Sabrina Bryan who plays Dorinda said about street youth in India, "The kids, it's their job every day to be there on the side of the street trying to ask for food and for money. It just makes you grateful. It's something every teenager should come and [see] to understand how much we have in the States." In this way, the Cheetah Girls serve as an example of benevolent texts that purport to teach us good things about other cultural groups and that ultimately sustain imperial relationships.

Implications for Literacy Education

As media literacy scholars suggest, the Cheetah Girls are not outside of formal schooling; rather, the pedagogies and pleasures within these texts are central to the work of literacy educators. Critical media literacy is an important approach for theorizing the Cheetah Girls as this case exemplifies an increasing number of texts produced for, marketed to, and/or consumed by tween girls. Often, pedagogical interventions for popular texts for tween girls focus on making girl readers/viewers aware of the "bad" sexist or sexualized messages contained within mainstream narratives. This often leads to gendered curricular interventions that Helen Harper (1998) defined as "rescue" projects in which young girls are saved from the harm of popular culture. She proposed an alternative approach in line with contemporary critical media literacy approaches:

> The English classroom needs to be a place to tolerate, invite, and interpret the complexity, ambiguity and contradiction that exist in text, and in our investments and identity formations as we negotiate with texts. The "rescue"

of students does not mean cutting a single new route of connection for our students but rather an experience that complicates current notions of identity and desire, thus producing and acknowledging a dense terrain with many complex routes possible.

(Harper, 1998, p. 226)

The pleasures of popular cultural texts lie in the fantasies and desires that circulate within them. In the Cheetah Girls' materials, that fantasy is organized around travel and benevolence and the opportunity to imagine oneself as a global-girl citizen. Thus, one of the ways to complicate the representation of girlhood within the Cheetah Girls case is to complicate the representation of this corporately produced global-gendered identity as one that is not just about gender.

The Cheetah Girls serve as just one example of ways in which global girlhood is used as a marketing tool that delineates and continues to play out the imperialistic binary of First World/Third World. Burns asked:

in imagining herself as adequately "global," how does the girl-citizen participate in certain political and cultural economies that allow her to consume experiences of non-White, Third World and Indigenous "others," and how is this consumption validated as part of her broader entrepreneurial agenda of global self-making?

(Burns, 2008, p. 354)

The Cheetah Girl materials, like other contemporary popular cultural texts aimed at the lucrative tween market, educate girl readers, viewers, and gamers that empowerment can be attained by consuming Other girlhoods through a range of technology and media. How we as educators decide to analyze and re-imagine these materials with students requires that we acknowledge the dense terrain of popular culture, media and youth.

References

Billboard (2003). Top Soundtracks. Billboard (serial online). November 22, 2003, 115(47), 64. Available from: Business Source Complete, Ipswich, MA. Accessed March 14, 2012.

Burns, K. (2008). "(re)Imagining the global, rethinking gender in education." *Discourse: Studies in the Cultural Politics of Education 29*, 343–357.

Campaign for a Commercial Free Childhood. "Marketing to Children Overview." http://www.commercialfreechildhood.org/factsheets/overview.pdf (Retrieved 05/05/2010.)

Castleberry, S.B. & Merrier, P.A. (2008). How young is too young? Marketing to the tween generation. *Journal of Business Case Studies 4*(1): 55–60.

duCille, A. (1994). Dyes and dolls: Multicultural Barbie and the merchandising of difference. *Differences: A Journal of Feminist Cultural Studies 16*(1), 46–68.

Grewal, I. (1996). *Home and harem: Nation, gender, empire and the cultures of travel.* Durham, NC: Duke University Press.

Harper, H. (1998). Dangerous desires: Feminist literary criticism in a high school writing class. *Theory into Practice 37*(3), 220–228.

Heffernan, V. (2006). A girl band in Spain fending off adulthood. *New York Times*, August 25, p. E19.

Jenkins, H. (2006). *Convergence culture: Where old and new media collide*. New York: New York University Press.

Jiwani, Y. (2006). *Discourses of denial: Mediations of race, gender, and violence*. Vancouver, BC: UBC Press.

Kearney, M.C. (2006). *Girls make media*. New York: Routledge.

Kellner, D. & Share, J. (2005). Toward critical media literacy: Core concepts, debates, organizations, and policy. *Discourse: Studies in the Cultural Politics of Education, 26*(3), 369–386.

Kellner, D. & Share, J. (2007). Critical media literacy, democracy, and the reconstruction of education. In *Media literacy: A reader* (pp. 3–23). New York: Peter Lang.

Lamb, S. & Brown, L.M. (2006). *Packaging girlhood: Rescuing our daughters from marketers' schemes*. New York: St Martin's Griffin.

Marshall, E. (2012). Global girl citizens and strangers: Marketing transnational girlhood through the Nancy Drew series. *Children's Literature Association Quarterly, 37*(2), 210–227.

Marshall, E. & Sensoy, Ö. (2011). *Rethinking popular culture and media*. Milwaukee: Rethinking Schools.

Prince, D. & Martin, N. (2011). The tween market niche: An overview of past research, current practices, and a comprehensive research model. In JoAnn Carland and Jim Carland (Eds.), *Proceedings of the Allied Academies' International Internet Conference*, Vol. 13, 2011 (pp. 95–98). Arden, NC: DreamCatchers Group.

Sensoy, Ö. & Marshall, E. (2010). Missionary girl power: Saving the "Third World" one girl at a time. *Gender and Education 22*(3), 295–311.

Staples, J. (2008). Hustle & Flow: A critical student and teacher-generated framework for re-authoring a representation of Black masculinity. *Educational Action Research 16*(3), 377–390.

Steinberg, S. & Kincheloe, J. (2004). *Kinderculture: The corporate construction of childhood*. 2nd ed. Boulder, CO: Westview Press.

Storey, J. (2009). *Cultural theory and popular culture: An introduction*. 5th ed. Harlow, Essex: Pearson Education Limited.

PART II

Gender Influences and Identities in New Literacies Practices

5

THE IMAGE YOU CHOOSE IS THE AVATAR YOU USE

Re-thinking Gender in New Literacies

Guy Merchant

Early in 2012, as part of an ongoing investigation into gang-related crime in London, the Metropolitan Police revealed alarming evidence of how young girls were using social networking sites to affiliate with gangs. The police claimed that girls, some as young as 13, were posting highly sexualized photographs to "advertise" themselves to older, male gang members (Taylor, 2012). These online practices contrasted starkly with the ways in which the male gang members would upload videos and pictures of themselves— often posing with weapons or boasting about their illicit activity. Stories like this illustrate how the new literacies associated with social networking sites (SNSs) become a public arena for diverse, and sometimes troubling, performances of identity.

In the highly-gendered social world of adolescence, in which self-consciousness and sensitivity to peer pressure is amplified, teenage girls often achieve status in their peer group through their associations with and attractiveness to young men (Thorne, 1993). Furthermore, in some segments of society, and in some localized networks, both status and a sense of security are achieved through gang affiliation (Miller, 2001). With the increased take-up of digital technology, it is perhaps predictable then, that these, and other gendered practices, are acted out in online environments. After all, new technologies are embedded within social structures and relations.

Clearly, performing gender online is no simple matter. First the very diversity of practices needs to be acknowledged. Studies, including my own (Merchant, 2001; 2010), depict teenage girls with very different sensibilities and sensitivities to those on the periphery of gang culture. These are young people with a different sense of audience, alternative ideas of what is appropriate online, and a keen sense of adult-defined notions of Internet safety. A complex picture of appropriateness, and who defines it, begins to emerge. Second, the rapid assimilation of SNSs into daily life, accelerated by the availability of sites like Facebook on mobile devices disturbs the boundaries between face-to-face and online activity. Often, the back and forth movement between the two is so rapid that they defy separation—what was said on Facebook, who texted who, and the latest celebrity tweets are seamlessly interwoven with face-to-face conversation. As a result, it becomes rather difficult to separate online gender performance from the social lives in which it is embedded.

But this is not quite the impression that some writing in the field of new literacies and digital culture creates. Often, the prevailing view is that online environments are in some way divorced from social context; that participants can happily shrug off everyday identities as they enter into an egalitarian communicative space. This utopian view has been regularly re-played in popular writing about social media (Rheingold, 2003; Shirky, 2008; Leadbetter, 2009), and it tends to obscure the ways in which both online and offline communication is patterned by social structure.

At the same time, however, influential theorists have pointed to important changes in our social world—changes that disrupt familiar notions of social structure. Writers like Giddens (1991) and Beck (1992) suggest that the current condition of late modernity is characterized by a more atomized social order in which the individual is more significant than the community or social group. This "individualization" thesis claims that changes in the labor market, the decline of heavy industry, increased globalization, and new patterns of family life are loosening our ties to neighborhood, nation, and class. The resultant weakening of traditional markers of identity means that individuals now have to do the work of creating their own "narrative of the self" (Giddens, 1991, p. 243). Building on this idea of individualization, it has been argued that Web 2.0 technologies, in the form of blogs, Facebook updates and tweets, demonstrate how the Internet provides a wealth of opportunities to produce and publish just the sort of ongoing autobiography of the self that Giddens describes (Davies & Merchant, 2007). In this way, the conditions of late modernity are reflected in digital communication.

Despite these changes in the social landscape, and the trend towards individualization, the intersections of gender, race, and class are still powerful influences, as the above story of online identity performance in gang subculture illustrates. Although globalization and the democratization of digital production may provide the conditions for the emergence of new femininities (Kehily & Nayak, 2008), traditional, and sometimes undesirable, gender politics still play out online (Herring et al., 2004). In this chapter, I argue for a re-thinking of the ways in which social contexts both shape, and are shaped by uses of technology and more particularly, for a renewed focus on how gender is performed in the new literacies of digital communication.

The New Literacies of Online Social Networking

The rapidly increasing popularity of online social networking is a telling indicator of changing levels of engagement with digitally-mediated communication. Over a relatively short period of time, online social networking has contributed to the normalization of Internet usage, and activities such as status-updating, picture-sharing, and tweeting have become woven into the very fabric of social interaction. Uptake has been widespread and transnational, while at the same time being unevenly distributed and locally interpreted (Consenza, 2011). Although the use of social networking sites spans many traditional social groupings, such as race, gender, social class, occupation and age, there is plenty of evidence of the barriers and limitations to participation, as well as carefully articulated resistance or refusal (Hargittai, 2008). Despite this, the reach of SNSs has become such that their role in the everyday social interactions and friendship groups of many sectors of the population—but perhaps, most notably amongst teenagers and young people—cannot be ignored.

For educators, this unparalleled explosion of everyday digital communication has provoked a range of reactions. SNSs have been vilified by some, who consider them to be a corrosive influence on friendship, on face-to-face interaction, and on standards of written communication (Palmer, 2006). Others have felt that SNSs belong to the informal world of students, and that any attempt by educators to recognize, discuss or use them in formal contexts amounts to a sort of colonization (Burnett & Merchant, 2011). Yet others have argued that the rise of social net-working provides important opportunities and challenges, as Hull & Stornaiuolo assert:

> the rewards could not be greater, or the risk of failure more grave for educating a citizenry able and willing to communicate with digital tools across differences in a radically interconnected yet divided world.
>
> *(Hull & Stornaiuolo, 2010, p. 85)*

In many ways, these different orientations rehearse familiar positions on the relationship between the popular culture of children and young people, and the more formal world of educational institutions. The distinctiveness of social media lies in the ways in which new literacies (Lankshear & Knobel, 2010) are implicated in new kinds of connectivity and emerging patterns of social organization. Social media are more or less unregulated communicative spaces in which boundaries between the formal and the informal, work and leisure, seriousness and frivolity have become blurred. They are also social spaces in which new multimodal practices that involve the orchestration of words, music, and still and moving image, are used as ways of producing and consuming ongoing performances of identity.

The new literacies are key to understanding the changing social order and particularly the ways in which youth position themselves, and are positioned by others. The observation that the "new matrix of gender and class, is articulated most clearly in and through the fields of culture and media" (McRobbie, 2002, p. 106) seems eminently applicable to the study of the new literacies of social networking. It is certainly not the case, however, that new technology *determines* a new economy of communication, or for that matter, that changing social relationships have *created* new technologies of communication, but that the two emerge together and are interconnected in complex ways.

Doing Gender in Social Networks: The Educational Concern

The relationship between literacy and identity has emerged as a key theme in recent scholarly writing (Merchant & Carrington, 2009; Moje et al., 2009). Literacy researchers and educators, and particularly those working in the socio-cultural tradition, have become increasingly interested in how literacy has become a significant site for identity work. Literacy practices, and particularly those associated with new media, provide an arena for experimenting with self-pre-sentation, and for creatively constructing or performing identities. Whether, and how, this creativity is taken up or constrained by notions of what is acceptable, by self-policing and surveillance is a topic I return to later. This is, nevertheless, a world in which young people are becoming literate across a range of social media and are regular participants in online environments—and this has implications for educators.

Greenhow and Robelia (2009, p. 136) in their investigation of high school students' online social networking conclude their report by suggesting that "educators must help students enact legal, ethical, responsible, safe and advan-tageous online community practices."

These researchers note that alongside issues about Internet safety, educators need to promote what they describe as *advantageous* practices. One of the challenges that emerges along with the concept of advantageousness is that of attribution. In the light of this, in my own work with Cathy Burnett, we have posed questions about *whose advantage* is served and *who defines* what constitutes advantage (Burnett & Merchant, 2011). For us, advantageous practices are those that contribute to: increasing individuals' life chances; enhancing civic engagement; empowerment through collaboration and participation; making a positive contribution to the wider community; and recognizing and responding to diverse identities and viewpoints.

We also argued for an approach that recognizes how identity is performed through specific practices that are framed in various ways—not only by the architecture and culture of SNSs, but also through wider online and offline activity. These performances are prompted by the design templates and practices associated with SNSs, as well as by the discourses that circulate as individuals connect to others and others connect to them (Burnett & Merchant, 2011, p. 51).

A final theme in the literature that relates to gender and new literacies is the patterning of preference and "conspicuous consumption" on SNSs. What is publicly displayed or consumed can be read as a symbolic marker of identity. The ethics and aesthetics of textual performance on profile pages has become an important focus for researchers, such as Liu (2008), who are interested in taste performance, patterns of consumption and related issues of impression management and self-presentation. In this way, cultural artifacts play a key role in online identity performance, as preferences of dress, music and popular narrative are curated for one's real, and imagined, audience.

Given these concerns, it seems important for educators to address students' engagement in SNSs. Elsewhere (Burnett & Merchant, 2011), I have suggested three different approaches that need to be explored in educational contexts. These are: (1) *learning about* SNSs and their role in learners' lives; (2) *learning from* SNSs, to appreciate new kinds of social interaction and informal learning; (3) *learning with* SNSs, making use of learners' existing online social networks to support and extend curriculum-based work. These considerations may begin to add to what might be seen as a critical approach to new literacy practices (Burnett & Merchant, 2011).

How Do I Look? The Student's Perspective

The densely connected relationships promoted by SNSs allow, and even encourage, users to anchor their relationships and social activities to the real world; this not only raises new and complex issues of privacy and self-expression (Livingstone, 2008), but also involves specific strategies for making connections and relationships visible. More often than not, the identity work done online has an iterative relationship with offline identity (see Dowdall, 2009). As a result, this complexity of identity anchorage inevitably relates to notions of place (both in an actual and a metaphorical sense) and belonging. Spencer-Oatey argues:

> Identity helps people "locate" themselves in social worlds. By helping to define where they belong and where they do not belong in relation to others, it helps to anchor them in their social worlds, giving them a sense of place.
>
> *(Spencer-Oatey, 2007, p. 642)*

This sense of location, however, is unlikely to be fixed—teenagers and young people are competent social actors, negotiating a sense of who they are within a landscape of competing discourses. Against arguments for the leveling effect of digital culture, it appears that the weight of a historical and social past is pervasive, and that performances of gender, race, and class are still very much in evidence as strong, structuring forces. These are aspects of identity to which one is strongly anchored. At the same time, however, they co-exist and intersect with a kaleidoscope of identifications (often related to media consumption and popular culture)— transient identities that may be relatively easier to make or remake (Merchant, 2006).

For teenagers, SNSs provide an arena for some quite public negotiations around masculinity, femininity, and sexuality. In my own work (Merchant, 2010), I reported how teenage girls regularly talked about their preoccupation with "wanting to look their best" in the pictures they displayed on Facebook. They had quite clear views of what was, and what was not acceptable or appropriate. Images that showed friends, humorous situations, and social occasions were deemed to be acceptable, whereas anything that seemed like *"posing,"* as a self-conscious display of attractiveness, or indeed any material that was overtly sexual in nature would attract criticism from their friends. Participants in my study were very keen to "look their best," but this seemed to describe a particular version of femininity— one that accentuated "prettiness" rather than sexuality. As one teenager put it, "pouting" in a photograph was frowned upon: "I never do because you look ridiculous." An awareness of how one is seen by others seems crucially important, and the public evaluation, or appreciation, that appears in comments can become a highly important source of feedback. This phenomenon is underlined in the work of Livingstone (2008) who quotes one teenager from her study as saying: "It's like quite nice, I think when people say you're pretty . . . I like it when they comment me because like it shows they care" (Livingstone, 2008, p. 401). Of course, when we compare this with the uses of SNSs in and on the periphery of gang culture, we see that very different rules apply. The mainly middle-class teenagers I worked with clearly had quite distinct ideas of how to locate themselves in their social worlds.

The teens I studied were also acutely aware of how online spaces like Facebook could be used to navigate the complex worlds of friendship and intimacy. Online and offline worlds interwove as SNSs were sometimes used for an opening gambit, to circumvent inhibitions, and to provide a starting point for more delicate interactions.

> I think you can make closer friends with people because by talking to them—maybe on Facebook, maybe on the chat thing—you might then have more confidence to talk to them in school or out—I think that can help where you do sort of get close to people—and then it is easier to talk to people.

Of course, the role of SNSs in overcoming reticence or shyness in face-to-face communication sits alongside the work that these teenagers do in friendship maintenance—online activities that are frequently referred to as "catching up." Although some commentators have been rather dismissive of the banal or frivolous activity that this communication involves, I would argue that the playfully social (Graham, 2008) is an important facet of these new textual worlds, and has, in fact, always been significant in human communication. This was well-illustrated when one of my interviewees described how she might maintain a "connection" with her friend:

with your really close friends—like with us—we just leave sort of stupid comments—like if we haven't seen each other in a couple of days because now we are at a different school—it's just we will be like "love you."

This extract illustrates that it is likely that there are not only broad gender differences at play, but also marked differences within and between social networks. For example, the teenagers in my study showed that they were acutely aware of a wider web audience, and reiterated some of the media stories that have drawn attention to the blurring of personal and professional boundaries. For example, my informants told me that caution should be exercised in deciding what to make public because "you hear those things about how like universities and employers look at it [Facebook]."

Online performances, just like the offline practices they are connected to, seem to be oriented toward an audience—a known or imagined other, to whom one is giving an account of oneself. As Butler argues:

An account of oneself is always given to another, whether conjured or existing . . . the very terms by which we give an account, by which we make ourselves intelligible to ourselves are not of our making. They are social in character, and they establish social norms, a domain of unfreedom and substitutability within which our "singular" stories are told.

(Butler, 2005, p. 21)

Implications for Literacy Education

Since the writing of authors like Turkle (1995) and Stone (1991), work on gender and identity online has failed to make a significant impact on the public imagination. In the normalization of digital communication, questions of identity largely turned on moral panics around safety, fraud, criminal deception and sexual exploitation. With the notable exception of pioneers such as boyd (2007), the routine and everyday ways in which individuals represent themselves in popular digital environments has received little attention. Yet, recent work in education that has focused on social networking has begun to revisit these questions (Greenhow & Robelia, 2009; Merchant, 2010; Hull & Stornaiuolo, 2010), suggesting that public education has an important role to play in encouraging children and young people to reflect upon what they do online, and why how they represent themselves to others.

Studies suggest that social media provide rich and supportive conditions for teenage girls to explore new femininities (e.g., Gómez, 2010; Lam, 2009; Thomas, 2004), but social media tend to assume a level of access and participation that is far from universal. The Internet is not a unitary phenomenon, digital communication is diverse, and online interaction is by its very nature plural. Although Web 2.0 environments present opportunities to produce an ongoing autobiography of the self, individuals who engage in this activity may well draw on existing templates of identity. The space for performing new femininities may be more constrained than once thought, and online communication may well be more routinely marked by gender. As Kehily and Nayak observe:

> Young women are increasingly positioned as the ideal neo-liberal subjects of late modernity—flexible, technologically savvy, open to change and in control of their own destiny. However, the contradictions of new media technologies are apparent where webcams, Skype and mobile phones may offer forms of communication and connectedness for young women but also can be seen as modern modes of governance and surveillance.
>
> *(Kehily & Nayak, 2008, p. 339)*

Furthermore, it seems that home and leisure uses of digital literacy often link to traditional socialization by gender (Koutsogiannis & Adampa, 2012). As a result, gendered identities are actively formed and reformed in online interaction. So although the idea of individualization, associated as it is with late modernity, has been influential in studies of digital communication, familiar gender formations are emerging from the dense web of social media.

Social contexts both shape, and are shaped by uses of technology. There is an urgent need for a renewed focus on how gender is performed in the new literacies of digital communication. If new literacies are characterized by new ways of producing, consuming, and distributing texts, descriptions of these rapidly changing communicative practices should not ignore the patterning of the meanings that circulate. Re-mixing is a familiar concept in new literacies (Lankshear & Knobel, 2010)—and in the context of the current debate, it is appropriate to ask "what is being re-mixed?" If the self-narratives of young people are just re-mixes of dominant and dominating discourses perhaps educators should be concerned.

In the new literacy practices of social media, teenagers often work as competent social actors, and they orchestrate a range of semiotic resources in largely unmoderated environments in which what is shown, as well as what is referenced, is just as important as what is said. This constitutes an educational challenge because while youth may sometimes have an active and skilled role in these spaces, they may just as easily become passive consumers, recycling old inequalities and stereotypes. I have argued that public education has an important role to play in introducing the kinds of reflexivity and criticality that will help students to act in ways that are ethical and advantageous. A useful pedagogic approach would be to move from a consideration and reflection on existing practices, and the identities that are performed within specific networks, to an examination of new practice possibilities. This would entail broadening out from questions about *what we are doing* in social media to a consideration of *what might we be doing* in social media. This would involve invoking goals and ambitions (both personal and social) to sit alongside the skills and competencies associated with new literacies.

References

Beck, U. (1992). *Risk society: Towards a new modernity*. London: Sage.

boyd, d. (2007). Why youth <3 social network sites: The role of networked publics in teenage social life. In: D. Buckingham (Ed.) *Youth identity and digital media*. Cambridge, MA: MIT Press (pp. 119–42).

Burnett, C. & Merchant, G. (2011). Is there a space for critical literacy in the context of new media? *English, Practice and Critique 10*(1), 41–57.

Butler, J. (2005). *Giving an Account of Oneself*. New York: Fordham University Press.

Consenza, V. (2011). World Map of Social Networks. Available at http://www.vincos. it/world-map-of-social-networks (Accessed February 28, 2012.)

Davies, J. & Merchant G. (2007). Looking from the inside out: Academic blogging as new literacy. In: C. Lankshear & M. Knobel (Eds.) *A new literacies sampler*. New York: Peter Lang (pp. 167–197).

Dowdall, C. (2009). Masters and critics: Children as producers of online digital texts. In V. Carrington & M. Robinson (Eds.) *Digital literacies: Social learning and classroom practice*. London: Sage (pp. 43–61).

Giddens, A. (1991). *Modernity and self-identity: self and society in the late modern age*. Oxford: Polity.

Gómez, A.G. (2010). Disembodiment and cyberspace: Gendered discourses in female teenagers' personal information disclosure. *Discourse & Society, 21*(2), 135–160.

Graham, L. (2008). Teachers are digikids too: The digital histories and digital lives of young teachers in English primary schools. *Literacy 42*(1), 10–18.

Greenhow, C. & Robelia, B. (2009). Informal learning and identity formation in online social networks, *Learning, Media and Technology, 34*(2), 119–140.

Greenhow, C., Robelia, B., & Hughes, J.E. (2010) Learning, teaching and scholarship in a digital age: Web 2.0 and classroom research: What path should we take now? *Educational Researcher, 38*(4), 246–259.

Hargittai, E. (2008). Whose space? Differences amongst users and non-users of social networking sites. *Journal of Computer-Mediated Communication 13*, 276–297.

Herring, S.C., Kouper, I., Scheidt, L.A., & Wright, E.L. (2004). Women and children last: The discursive construction of weblogs.' Available at http://blog.lib.umn.edu/blogo sphere/women_and_children.html (Accessed February 28, 2012.)

Hull, G.A. & Stornaiuolo, A. (2010). Literate arts in a global world: Reframing social networking as a cosmopolitan practice, *Journal of Adolescent & Adult Literacy, 54*(2), 85–97.

Kehily, M. & Nayak, A. (2008). Global femininities: Consumption, culture and the significance of place. *Discourse: Studies in the Cultural Politics of Education, 29*(3), 325–342.

Koutsogiannis, D. & Adampa, V. (2012). Girls, identities and agency in adolescents' digital literacy practices. *Journal of Writing Research, 3*(3), 217–247.

Lam, W. (2009). Multiliteracies on instant messaging in negotiating local, translocal and transnational affiliations: A case of an adolescent immigrant. *Reading Research Quarterly 44*(4), 377–397.

Lankshear, C. & Knobel, M. (2010). *New literacies: Everyday practices and social learning* (3rd ed.). Maidenhead: Open University Press.

Leadbetter, C. (2009). *We-think: Mass innovation not mass production*. London: Profile Books.

Liu, H. (2008). Social network profiles as taste performances. *Journal of Computer-Mediated Communication 13*, 252–275.

Livingstone, S. (2008). Taking risky opportunities in youthful content creation: Teenagers' use of social networking sites for intimacy, privacy and self-expression. *New Media & Society, 10*(3), 393–411.

McRobbie, A. (2002). Notes on "What not to wear" and postfeminist symbolic violence. *Sociological Review 52*(2), 97–109.

Merchant, G. (2001). Teenagers in cyberspace: An investigation of language use and language change in internet chatrooms. *Journal of Research in Reading, 24*(3), 293–306.

Merchant, G. (2006). Identity, social networks and online communication. *E-Learning, 3*(2), 235–244.

Merchant, G. (2010). View my profile(s). In D.Alvermann (Ed.) *Adolescents' online literacies.* New York: Peter Lang.

Merchant, G. & Carrington, V. (2009). Literacy and identity. *Literacy 43*(2), 63–64.

Miller, J. (2001). *One of the guys: Girls gangs and gender.* New York: Oxford University Press.

Moje, E., Luke, A., Davies, B., & Street, B. (2009). Literacy and identity: Examining the metaphors in history and contemporary research.' *Reading Research Quarterly 44*(4), 415–437.

Palmer, S. (2006). *Toxic childhood: How modern life is damaging our children and what we can do about it.* London: Orion.

Rheingold, H. (2003). *Smart mobs: The next social revolution.* Cambridge, MA: Perseus.

Shirky, C. (2008). *Here comes everybody: How change happens when people come together.* London: Penguin Books.

Spencer-Oatey, H. (2007). Theories of identity and the analysis of face. *Journal of Pragmatics 39*(4), 639–656.

Stone, S. (1991). Will the real body please stand up? Boundary stories about virtual cultures. In M. Benedikt (Ed.) *Cyberspace: First steps.* Cambridge, MA: MIT Press.

Taylor, M. (2012). Young girls using Facebook to "advertise" to older gang members. *Guardian*, February 19, 2012. Available at http://www.guardian.co.uk/society/2012/feb/19/young-girls-facebook-advertise-gang-members (Accessed March 1, 2012.)

Thomas, A. (2004). Digital literacies of the cybergirl. *E-Learning, 1*(3), 358–382.

Thorne, B. (1993). *Gender play: Girls and boys in school.* New Brunswick, NJ: Rutgers University Press.

Turkle, S. (1995). *Life on the screen: Identity in the age of the internet.* New York: Simon & Schuster.

6

GIRLS' ZINES AS A GLOBAL LITERACY PRACTICE

Stories of Resistance and Representation

Barbara J. Guzzetti

Researchers have documented how girls take up gendered notions of femininity through their consumption of popular culture media texts such as commercial magazines marketed to young women that position them as passive objects of desire conforming to Western notions of beauty (Finders, 1997). Adolescent girls in the United States have voiced complaints about how women are represented in the classical literature that they study in school as minor characters, victims or incompetent people (Guzzetti & Gamboa, 2003). These gendered representations impact women across the globe both socially and politically (Peterson & Runyan, 2010).

While commercial and academic texts perpetuate stereotypical or gendered interpretations of women's roles, young women network globally to resist such notions by authoring independent publications known as zines (Knobel & Lankshear, 2001). Zines are underground publications that are self-authored and self-edited to allow those who often remain unheard to be recognized. Through zining, young women take up topics of importance to them and have their voices heard on issues that are typically not written about in the popular press. As such, zines are a form of alternative media (Poletti, 2005).

Zines were first crafted in the 1930s as extensions of science fiction comics that served as a form of communication between science fiction fans. The 1990s brought the riot grrrl movement's reactions against sexism in punk rock, the rise of third-wave feminism that rejects a single view of feminism and embraces diversity and contradictions among feminists, the development of girl culture, and an increased interest in the do-it-yourself lifestyle (McDonald, 2006). It was during this decade that the women's and girls' zine culture began to thrive.

Today, zines can take myriad forms, ranging from a jumble of personal thoughts to expertly designed political discourse (McDonald, 2006). Zines' style is cut and paste, pastiche, or collage (Knobel & Lankshear, 2001). Their unifying theme is their outside-of-the-mainstream existence as independently written, produced, and distributed media with creators (both female and male) called zinesters who value freedom of expression (McDonald, 2006). Zinesters often craft their zines as rebellion against commercial texts. Their zines are a means of self-representation that enable relative strangers to communicate with one another (Duncombe, 1997).

My past collection of zines was conducted a decade ago. Since then, I have found that with the advent of Web 2.0, more zines are being promoted through electronic communications. In this new digital age, zinesters are linking their zines to their social networking sites, such as Ning, MySpace or Facebook and advertise them through online resources. Zines are now the subject of blogs, like the Newspapers Blog (http://newspapersblog.blogspot.com), and tweets on Twitter, a micro-blogging and social-networking tool. Zines are being tied to their creators' social networking sites as group memberships (e.g., *We Make Zines*). These technologies that have arisen in the new millennium enable international awareness and dissemination of zines.

Prior research on zines and the act of producing zines (zining) has been mostly confined to analyzing zines produced in the USA and has not focused on girls' zines (e.g., Guzzetti & Gamboa, 2003; Knobel & Lankshear, 2001). Most studies of zines were conducted by researchers examining zines as literacy practices within North America. Researchers have tended to confine their efforts to identifying the types of zines young people produce and describing their diverse formats and contents.

Yet, there is evidence that zines have become a global means of communication, particularly among young women (Zobl, 2004). More than a decade ago, Duncombe (1997) in his dissertation research located zines from 24 countries, identifying zinesters in the major English-speaking nations, such as Canada (58 zines); the UK (37 zines); and Australia (13 zines). Today, international zine festivals and workshops are thriving in forums like the Festival of the Photocopier, held in Melbourne, Australia, celebrating Australia's underground zine culture (http://www.pretty-ugly.com); Portland, Oregon's annual zine symposium (http://pdxzines.com); the Brighton, England Zinefest (http://www.brighton zinefest.co.uk); and Saskatchewan's Council for International Cooperation DIY project, sponsoring young people making zines on global issues (http://zinewiki. com/Youth_for_International_Development).

Cross-national repositories have been created to promote and house zines known as "distros." International distros offer zines from various nations, such as the Fat Cheeks Distro and the Sticky Institute (http://stickyinstitute.com) in Australia that exchanges zines with Micrcosom Distro (http://micrcosom publishing, com) in Portland, Oregon; Moon Rocket Distribution in New Zealand; You and Me in Croatia; the Marching Stars and Vampire Sushi distros in the United Kingdom; and the Passionate Résistance distro from Germany (http://www.slcpl.lib.ut.us/details.jsp?parent_id=134&page_id174). In addition, zine libraries have archived zines, such as the Salt Lake City Public Library Alternative Press (http://www.slcpl.lib.ut.us) and the Denver Zine Library (www.geocities.com/denverzinelibrary). Zines are distributed at "infoshops" (a space that combines a movement archive with a radical bookstore), such as the Insight Infoshop in Eau Claire, Wisconsin (inforshop@angelfire.com). Zines are also archived at colleges and universities, like Barnard College, San Diego State University, and the University of Montana. Zines are sold at minimal cost on Etsy (http://www.etsy.com), a global online marketplace for handmade items.

Girls' zines have been characterized as artifacts of a long tradition of counter-hegemonic print media (Kearney, 2006). Feminist practice emphasizes the sharing of personal experience for community building. Zines have proven to be the perfect medium for reaching out to young women across the globe as a means of revolution and resistance (McDonald, 2006). Zines have been credited for supporting and advancing the transnational nature of the Riot Grrrl movement, a feminist punk community that explores systemic problems of patriarchy and heterocentrism (Kearney, 2006). The three angry "rs" like growls in the word "Grrrl" reflect the rebellious reclamation of the word "girl" and signal identification with the alternative feminist community (Zobl, 2004) advanced by zining. The Grrrl Zine Network (http://grrrlzines.net/overview.htm) serves as a repository for and a source of information about feminist Riot Grrrl zines.

Researchers who examined young women's zines (Harris, 2003; Kearney, 2006; Schilt, 2003) tended to restrict their analysis to feminist zines as social media for activism, and focused in particular on Riot Grrrl zines (http://grrrlzines.net/writingonzines.htm). These zines are forms of resistance against patriarchical notions of females in competition with each other. By emphasizing the cooperative, these zines have served as vehicles for feminist community building, support, and networking (Currie et al., 2009; Kearney, 2006; Zobl, 2004).

Although grrrl zines are known for establishing connectivity on a global scale, researchers have also called for an examination of girls' zines as tools for identity expression (Guzzetti & Gamboa, 2004; Kearney, 2006). Zining allows zinesters to explore and experiment with new identities. Although zines have been recognized as artifacts of girl power culture (Currie et al., 2009) they have also been recognized as vehicles for young women to try on and test out new identities (Kearney, 2006). Research on girls' zines as a global literacy practice is now needed that constitutes a more inclusive agenda, particularly in terms of origin, topic, and type.

My Purpose

I wanted to draw attention to the topics, issues, and concerns raised by young women across the globe in enacting their identities as females in the 21st century. My goal was to analyze zines produced by young women as a global literacy practice, including but not restricting the analysis to feminist zines. I sought to identify both commonalities and uniqueness in zines produced by young women globally, and to describe the ways in which young women take up this new literacy practice to foster glocality and individuality, and provide implications for literacy instruction.

Perspectives

I analyzed the zines I collected from multiple and complementary theoretical perspectives. The first of these was literacy as a social practice (Street, 1995). This position illuminates the importance of studying adolescents' out-of-school literacy practices, those literacy practices that they engage in by choice. Since adolescence is a time of self-discovery, girls and young women use communicative practices in social ways to help them test out and try on new identities (Gee, 1996).

Two complementary views of feminism also informed this project. The first of these was feminist poststructuralism (Butler, 1990). This theory is commonly associated with the work of French theorist, Michel Foucault and has the analytical agenda of deconstructing power relationships (Luke, 2001). Feminist post-structuralism critiques structuralists' accounts of dichotomous gender differences and deconstructs the patriarch that has repressed women's voices, subjectivity, and opportunities (Luke, 2001). Foucault (1983) described power as a mode of action where discourse is an act of power. Zining has been considered to be an act of power or civil disobedience that balks at the societal demand that girls should not speak their minds (http://www.Columbia.edu%Ekw139/activism.html).

A second view of feminism that informed my analysis was a feminist sociology (Stanley & Wise, 1993). This perspective recognizes that multiple subjectivities interact with gender, like social class, generation, geographical location, sexual orientation, and culture. This theory asserts that men in their interactions with women are worthy of study, a belief that allowed collection and examination of zines that might be coauthored, co-edited or co-contributed to by both females and males.

The Zines

From these perspectives, I collected zines from multiple sources. Locating girls' zines from outside the United States was a more daunting task than I anticipated. Of the dozen international feminist grrrl zines and distros that Zobl identified in 2004, only one zine and its collective (*Pretty Ugly* from Australia) was currently accessible in 2010. The online distros that I located by referral from a local zinester included titles and descriptions of zines, but did not identify their country of origin. Zines produced internationally were often sold out, expensive, or inaccessible. Lists of zine distros on Wikipedia (http://en.wikipedia.org/wiki/list_of_zine_

distros) provided no contact information. Zines from an online distro I located in the United Kingdom, Corn Dog Publishing (http://www.CornDog.co.uk/zine-distro) were often no longer available or written in another language. Like Schilt (2003), I discovered that since zining is an underground practice, zines are fugitive documents.

I also discovered that the zine community now includes more young men than I encountered in the past. A tally of zines produced by young men on the distro, False-Start (www.false-start.com), showed that of the first 360 zines described on this site, 3 were coauthored by a male and a female, and 87 were done by zinesters whose gender was undeterminable. Of the remaining 270, the majority (161) were edited or authored by young men.

Given these limitations, I gathered a sample of 11 print zines created by females from two popular online distros, Microcosm Publishing (http://microcosm publishing.com) and False Start (http://www.false-start.com). I chose zines that from their titles and descriptions reflected a range of the types of zines young women produce, including three feminist zines, four themed zines (zines devoted to one topic), and four personal zines of poetry, art, prose, or cartoons. I focused particularly on zines produced by young women who were late adolescents or had recently left chronological adolescence, ranging from their late teens to their mid 20s as revealed in their zine's distro descriptions, writings, or interviews with their creators.

Titles I selected from Microcosm included: *Memoirs of a Queer Hapa, Issue 2*, from Sarasota, Florida, pieces written during different periods in a biracial, lesbian life and her impressions as an American-born Chinese (ABC) as she traveled around the world; *Radical Pet, Issue 5*, a DIY (do-it-yourself) guide to homeopathic health care for pets compiled by a young woman in Sparks, Maryland; *Tenacious: Art and Writings from Women in Prison, Issue 17*, articles, poetry, and art created for and sent free of charge to incarcerated women, edited in New York City; *Going Postal, Issue 2*, a zine edited by a young woman from Caceres, Spain devoted to the history of the overlapping movements of zines and mail art; and *Not Your Mother's Meatloaf: A Sex Education Comic Book* coauthored by two young women in Brooklyn, New York.

I also gathered five zines from the False-Start distro: *DIY or Don't We? Issue 1*, a zine about identity-based communities and DIY living from Olympia, Washington; *Ker-Bloom, Issue 77*, a letterpress-printed zine written by a member of an all-lady rock band from Pittsburg, Pennsylvania; *Shotgun Seamstress, Issue 2*, a zine edited by and for Black girls who are punk and/or queer and the people who support them from Portland, Oregon; *Manderz Totally Top Private Diary, Issue 2*, a diary comic written by a lesbian from San Francisco; and *Stab and Root #7* from two young women writing about their experiences establishing a zine library and infoshop in Halifax, Nova Scotia in Canada.

In addition to these print zines, I located, printed, and archived two issues of a Riot Grrrl e-zine, *Pretty Ugly, Issues 1 and 2* from a young woman in Melbourne,

Australia (http://ww.pretty_ugly.com). I also collected and printed interviews with this zinester, and three other feminist zinesters archived on the *Global Girl Zine Network*, an Internet compendium of zines and distros from across the world. These included interviews with the creators of *Grrrl Rebel*, a zine co-edited by a 23-year-old Malaysian female living in Australia and a 24-year-old female from southern Malaysia; and *Good Girl!*, edited by a 25-year-old female from Toronto, Canada. I also perused information on and posts to the site's electronic discussion list.

I conducted informal interviews by email with two of the zinesters whose zines I collected. I interviewed the creator of the diary-comic zine, *Manderz Totally Top Private Diary* from San Francisco, and the creator of the Riot Grrl zine, *Pretty Ugly* from Australia. These interviews focused on determining the zinesters' demographic information, zining history, and intent. I asked these young women what function zining served in their lives and what they were currently doing with zining.

I also examined several Internet sources on zines. I joined the social networking site, *We Make Zines* at http://www.wemakezines.ning.com, an online community for zine makers and readers. This site allows a member to create a profile, list his or her zineography, post images of zines, partake in discussion forums, find other zinesters, read about new releases and reviews from favorite zinesters, and post comments about zines on the actual zinester's profile. This site was linked to a MySpace group which I also joined. In addition, I became a member of the *Pander Zine Distro* group on Facebook, a distro devoted to grrrl and lady zines from all over the world. The distro is no longer in existence, but the social networking group discusses zines, new distros, and zine events.

Finally, I searched two websites devoted to zines. These included *Zines by Women and Girls: A Resource Pathfinder* (http://www.ils.unc.edu/%7Eophelia2/grrrlzines/index.html) and the *Salt Lake City Public Library Alternative Press* (http://www.slcpl.lib.ut.us/details.jsp?parent_id=145&page_id+174). Each of these sites provided links to general information about zines, zine libraries, and zine distros.

My Analysis of Zines

I conducted a content analysis of the zines I collected by using techniques of thematic analysis (Patton, 1990). I read and reread each of the zines' contents. I annotated the prose, cartoons, poetry, and narratives in the zines by noting key words that signaled topics and assigning codes and subcodes that were later collapsed to form categories. Reoccurring categories became assertions or themes. I analyzed the interviews, websites, and social networking sites in much the same way. In reporting my results, I have used pseudonyms for the zinesters unless I was given permission to use their actual names.

Resistance

The act of zining in itself has been considered to be an act of resistance against the silencing and loss of voice that young women experience beginning in adolescence (Schilt, 2003). Zining is a form of overt resistance that allows girls to express their anger, confusion, and frustration publicly to their peers (Schilt, 2003). Although zining has been considered to be a strategy of resistance (Harris, 2003; Schilt, 2003), few have examined girls' zines to identify other strategies of opposition they foster.

Strategies for Resistance: Love

Personal and feminist zines reflected a dominant theme of resistance against gender and sexual oppression. One of the ways zinesters took up resistance was by identifying specific strategies for resistance. Love was a common strategy for resistance identified by zinesters, particularly self-love. For example, in *Memoirs of a Queer Hapa*, a young woman from Florida, Janie Chang, writes for and about resistance, chronicling her experiences growing up bi-racial while living in the USA and China. The word "Hapa" in her zine's title, a Hawaiian word that literally means "half" is a term that has recently been taken up by activists and writers who are of mixed race and of Asian descent (Fulbeck et al., 2008). As a Hapa, Chang chronicles 15 reasons why love is important for mixed-race, queer people as a strategy to resist against society's oppression that fosters self-hatred. These included suppression of specific aspects of one's identity that results in loss of culture, language, and heritage; the need to choose between inadequate categories to be acknowledged; and the impact of ambiguous sexuality, gender representation, or race that makes others wary. Chang reminds her readers of the diversity and complexities of identity. Her zine provides a space for deconstructing the binary categories of difference that serves to limit enactment of multiple subjectivities of gender, race, sexual identity, and social class. Her zine has allowed her to articulate complexity and dissent, and critique of images of femininity and girlhood (Harris, 2003). Chang describes self-hatred as a manifestation of racism, sexism, homophobia, transphobia, classism, sizeism, and ableism (discrimination against those with disabilities) that weakens the ability to resist. Chang advocates doing love as an action:

> If you truly want to . . . bring down the system, learn to love. Love is one of the highest forms of resistance. If you can love yourself with the world mounted against you, you've truly accomplished something. Loving yourself and others happens simultaneously; it spreads; it enriches our communities; it makes the fight worthwhile.

In Chang's view, achieving self-love and self-respect can be accomplished by self- determination. Her zine is filled with action verbs, such as "struggle" ("we struggle to achieve self love"); "strive" ("we must strive for radical self love"); "fight" ("to fight the system we must truly reject the dominant value system"). These terms imply self-love as an overt action for resistance against society's stereotypes of proper roles for women and the enactment of femininity. Chang complains that many activist communities are devoid of love, focusing on accomplishing tasks rather than making individuals feel cared for as people. She posits that loving one's self and others can create communities of compassion that are open and organic while creating a culture of activism that is intimate and transformative.

Others zining for social justice also use the word "love," but tend to use it as a noun. Love is written about as a defense mechanism in the war against society's *repression of difference* that causes self-recrimination and loss of self-esteem. For example, in, *Shotgun Seamstress,* a young woman who is Black, queer, and a member of the punk community acquaints the reader with RuPaul, a famous Black, gay drag queen who alludes to reclaiming self-worth and self-esteem by using love to resist against society's oppressive value system. Self-love is a tool for establishing and maintaining self-esteem, a means of resistance against gendered, racist, and homophobic notions.

These zines illustrate a new kind of zinester within the zine community. Zinesters have tended to be White, middle-class young people who take up concerns and issues of their own ethnicity, race, social class, and culture (Schilt, 2003). This zine represents a new inclusivity. This zine illustrates that Grrrl and queer zines can overlap, and includes those females who produce alternative culture, but are often forgotten—queer, lesbian, bisexual, transgendered, and intersex youth (Zoble, 2004).

Strategies for Resistance: Coping Mechanisms

Zinesters writing in personal zines trouble oppression beyond the gender and sexual oppression written about by feminists, expanding the types of marginalized women who produce zines. Other new voices are being heard in the zine community—voices of incarcerated women who write of *repression of difference* stemming from society's views of women serving time. These zinesters wrote of strategies for resistance against oppression by a society that marginalizes them and the resulting self-loathing women experience when "doing time." Zinesters like Diane Nagy, a prisoner in the Hiland Mountain Correctional Center in Eagle River, Arkansas shared nine coping strategies for resistance: doing one day and one minute at a time; banishing self-pity; taking care of the body; stimulating the mind; working; becoming educated; being respectful and careful in placing trust; helping others; and finding a spiritual path.

Empowerment

The act of zining has been considered to be a strategy of girl empowerment (Schilt, 2003), creating a supportive community to aid girls in speaking out. Zining gives girls a safe space to practice articulating their thoughts and feelings and can assist in creating political action, as represented in a themed zine, *Stab and Root*. Two zinesters wrote about establishing the Anchor Archive in Halifax, a nonprofit organization devoted to zines and the DIY movement. These young women became activists for the DIY community by obtaining Canadian government grants to support zining. To disseminate zines, these zinesters established the Anchor Archive Radio Zine (http://www.CKDU.CA) that showcases zines. They wrote against gentrification in the north end of Halifax, taking up the cause of indigenous residents who are working-class and Black, forced out of their neighborhoods by higher taxes and rents associated with the influx of middle-class, transient students and artists suburbanizing this urban area. Other zinesters who personified empowerment in their zines included the editor of *Pretty Ugly* from Australia, Kathy. Kathy's zine is housed within a distro of the same name, supported by a grant she obtained from the Australian Arts Council Literature Board to produce the zine and maintain a related website. This zine and the collective allowed a space for young women to explore their ideas of feminisms.

Implications for Literacy Instruction

These zinesters serve as reminders that with increasing global immigration, young people today represent both U.S.-born and immigrant populations, and reflect increasing diversity. Therefore, a more flexible understanding of adolescence that recognizes and accounts for the social contexts and experiences of students by gender, class, and ethnicity must inform instruction. As Heilman (1998) noted more than a decade ago, relevant instruction needs to include discussion of issues that affect girls' sense of power. These discussions need to occur when relating to novels in English class, examining events in history, or using textbooks that lack representation of women's contributions. Content literacy instruction must include teaching to take critical perspectives. Lessons can be learned from zining in using writing to interrogate and undermine the dominant paradigms by which girls lives are commonly represented.

Finally, literacy instruction must recognize the myriad writing styles and modes that young people across the globe engage in as they author their lives. Today's millennial youth write in hybrid textual forms that combine or incorporate electronic texts, links, graphics, collage, and print mediums. They are writing for and with each other in collaborative ways to represent their multiple identities and facilitate global communication. These twenty-first-century writing skills and abilities should be recognized and fostered in classrooms globally to enable young people to network in new literate ways.

References

Butler, J. (1990). *Gender trouble: Feminism and the subversion of identity.* New York: Routledge.

Currie, D.H., Kelly, D.M., & Pomerantz, S. (2009). *Girl power: Girls reinventing girlhood.* New York: Peter Lang.

Duncombe, S. (1997). *Notes from the underground: Zines and the politics of alternative culture.* London: Verso.

Finders, M. (1996). Queens and teen zines: Early adolescent females reading their way toward adulthood. *Anthropology & Education Quarterly, 27*(1), 71–89.

Finders, M. (1997). *Just girls: Hidden literacies and life in junior high.* New York: Teachers College Press.

Foucault, M. (1983). The subject and power. In Dryphus, H.L. & Rabinow, P. (Eds.) *Michel Foucault: Beyond hermeneutics and structuralism* (pp. 208–226). Chicago: University of Chicago Press.

Fulbeck, K., Spickard, P. & Lennon, S. (2008). *Part Asian, 100% Hapa.* San Francisco, CA: Chronicle Books.

Garrison, E.K. (2001). U.S. Feminism—Grrrl style! Youth (sub)culture and the technology of the third wave. *Feminist Studies, 26*(1) 141–170.

Gee, J.P. (1996) *Social linguistics and literacies: Ideology in discourses,* 2nd ed. New York: Bergen & Garvey.

Guzzetti, B.J. & Gamboa, M. (2003). Zines for social justice: Adolescent girls writing on their own. *Reading Research Quarterly, 39*(4) 408–435.

Guzzetti, B.J. & Gamboa, M. (2004). Zines for social justice: Adolescent girls writing on their own. *Reading Research Quarterly 39*(4), 408–435.

Harris, A. (2003). gURL scenes and girl zines: The regulation and resistance of girls in late modernity. *Feminist Review 35*, 38–56.

Heilman, E.E. (1998). The struggle for self: Power and identity in adolescent girls. *Youth and Society, 30*(2) 182–208.

Kearney, M.C. (2006). *Girls make media.* New York: Routledge.

Knobel, M. & Lankshear, V. (2001). *Cut, paste, publish: The production and consumption of zines.* In D.E. Alvermann (Ed.) Adolescents and literacies in a digital world, (pp. 164–185). New York: Peter Lang.

Labovitz, J. (209). *About the e-zine list.* Retrieved April 5, 2009 from http://www.e-zine-list.com/about.shtml

Luke, C. (2001). Feminist poststructuralism. In B Guzzetti (Ed.), *Literacy in America: An encyclopedia of history theory and practice,* (pp. 187–191). Santa Barbara, CA: ABC-CLIO.

McDonald, A. (2006). *Zines by women and grrrls: A resource pathfinder.* Retrieved April 6, 2008 from http://www.ils.unc.edu/%7Eophelia2/grrrlzines/index.html

Patton, (1990). *Qualitative evaluation and research methods,* 2nd ed. Newbury Park, CA: Sage.

Peterson, V.S. & Runyan, A.S. (1993). *Global gender issues,* 2nd ed. Boulder, CO: Westview Press.

Peterson, V.S. & Runyan, A.S. (2010). *Global gender issues in the new millennium.* Boulder, CO: Westview Press.

Poletti, A. (2005). Self publishing in the global and the local: Situating life writing in zines. *Biography: An Interdisciplinary Quarterly 28*(1), 183–192.

Schilt, K. (2003). "I'll resist with every inch and breath:" Girls and zine making as a form of resistance. *Youth & Society, 35*(1), 71–97.

Stanley, L. & Wise, (1993). *Breaking out again: Feminist ontology and epistemology.* London: Routledge.

Street, B.V. (1995). *Social literacies.* New York: Longman.

Zobl, E. (2004). The power of pen publishing: International grrrl zines and distros. *Feminist Collections, 26*(1), 20–24.

Zoble, E. (2004). Persephone is pissed: Grrrl zine reading making and distributing across the globe. *Hecate, 30*(3), 156–176.

7

LITERACIES, IDENTITIES, AND GENDER

Reframing Girls in Digital Worlds

Cheryl A. McLean

In many ways, awareness of the connections to the "world" is far more immediate and real for today's millennial youth as they increasingly find themselves navigating global and local contexts brought about by migration, digital technologies and virtual spaces. For such youth, the "world" is simultaneously local and global, digital and technological, physical and virtual, and native and adopted. In particular, for immigrant youth, global-local tensions of multicultural contexts, and diverse literacy practices often mediate how their identities are co-constructed and positioned within their various communities. This is not to say that global-local realities, particularly for immigrant youth, are new (Stritikus & Nguyen, 2007); rather, the accelerated movement of peoples, ideas, and literacy practices across borders (Luke, 2004) brings a dynamic dimension to the understanding of immigration, identity and literacy. The ways in which gender identity shapes traditional renderings of students' word-world contexts suggests that our ongoing understanding of youth needs to be reframed within contemporary realities. In this chapter, I focus on the intersection of digital literacy practices and selfhood through the experiences of two immigrant high school girls in the United States. I explore the various ways in which two female, Caribbean immigrant adolescents inscribe their gender identities using digital literacies and networks in response to their globalized contexts.

Digital Literacy as Social Practice

Literacy in contemporary society has been re-conceptualized with the increasing dominance of digital technology and relatively fast-paced and easy flow of information and movement of peoples. A more inclusive view of literacy takes into account multiple ways of knowing and tools and modes of communication, including digital and online networks such as social networking sites, blogs, zines, instant messaging and video. In so doing, the expanded view helps shape and transform the contemporary social and educational landscapes by (re)defining "what count as 'acceptable' identities, actions and ways of knowing" (Gee, 1999, p. 356).

Critical Literacy

Critical literacy is a consciousness and a call to action. It involves the willingness to question, challenge and critique the power of inherited and oppressive beliefs, values and ideologies associated with language, texts and social contexts (Freire & Macedo, 1995). Critical literacy provides a lens from which to understand how the adolescents re-inscribe and re-present gendered identities in their various social networks. The individual not only uses literacy practices to communicate and operate within her communities, but also to purposively signal and actively use her literacies as a change agent. When this occurs, we see evidence of the individual's abilities to question, challenge, critique, and redefine beliefs. In this chapter, critical literacy can be seen as (1) involving a language of critique and the exercise of power, (2) allowing for authentic dialogue, and (3) focusing on the individual's experiences as participants in and creators of their social worlds (Freire, 1987; Comber & Kamler, 1997; Morrell, 2004).

Situating Gendered Identity

Identity-construction is a process that involves negotiating and organizing the self around discourses and practices with the aid of cultural resources and relationships (Holland et al., 1998). Gender is constituted through interactions and institutions: "it is a situated doing, carried out in the virtual or real presence of others who are presumed to be oriented to its production" (West & Zimmerman, 1987, p. 126). In this sense, *doing* gender involves acting, speaking, behaving, etc. in ways that constitute us as masculine or feminine. Taken together, gendered identity social discourses and practices have the power to position individuals around specific practices and dominant cultural ideologies that can exist online (Williams, 2007).

Situating the Study

This chapter focuses specifically on the experiences of two adolescent sisters, and the explicit connections they make between their online social networks and their gendered and ethnic identities as immigrant youth and females. The data were drawn from a year-long ethnographic study of first-generation Caribbean immigrant girls in the U.S.

Four years before, two sisters, Kai and Sade (pseudonyms) and their family had migrated from Jamaica to the U.S. At the time of the study, 17-year-old Sade and

14-year-old Kai were living in a metropolitan city in the U.S. south. Sade attended a public high school while Kai was a student at a private middle school. The family had made the decision to migrate for the purpose of "education" and "opportunities," and both siblings openly expressed their commitment to the decision. Each sibling used digital technology and online social networks as an integral part of her life. From Facebook to blogs, to zines, the two girls communicated, interacted, and learned via digital technology: they participated in social networking sites, completed schoolwork online, blogged, created podcasts, iMovies, and shopped online.

Data were collected using ethnographic research methods that included multiple individual interviews, and participants' digital texts and artifacts from social networking sites. Using samples from the participants' digital worlds, such as Facebook and blogs, along with interview transcripts, I consider how their digital worlds provide opportunities for these young women to co-construct and position their gendered selves. Using thematic analysis (Miles & Huberman, 1994; Ryan & Bernard, 2003) of the digital artifacts and interviews, recurring themes were identified that were linked to the research question and theoretical framework. The question guiding the analysis focused on how digital worlds shaped gender-identity.

Findings and Discussion

Through initial analyses of the data, the two adolescents can be seen to purposefully use their technological literacies to cultivate relationships to bridge cultural and social practices between H/homes (native and adopted homes) (McLean, 2010). The gendered self is positioned within and played out through their digital practices in the virtual communities and social networks via (1) the body, (2) advocating for self and others, and (3) (re)contextualizing language.

The Body

> The girls at school were totally different. They were into boys and stuff and I wasn't. These girls called me some name. And, I just thought it was so bizarre like these girls would like, try and pick a fight with me because we didn't really have a sense of fashion. These girls were like so into it [fashion]. In Jamaica, you know . . . I had uniforms for most of my whole life basically . . . Now, they say we dress preppy-ish.
>
> *(Sade)*

Normative practices, attitudes, and expectations associated with *being* female are reflected in how the body is presented and displayed. Sade finds herself negotiating cultural and gender norms in relation to the body and the ways in which girls are socialized about their physical self/appearance. Based on her initial experiences as a newcomer, and the negative responses by her U.S. peers to her cultural/family way of dressing she eventually redefines her gender identity by conforming to mainstream/normative values and views of the body by changing her ways of dressing to match that of her peers. Indeed, Sade's stance can be considered acculturation because she adapts to and adopts an approach to dressing that is considered acceptable, and "normal." Yet, her decision to conform can also be seen from another perspective: her actions are a conscious form of self-regulating in which she actively "monitor[s] her own and others' conduct with regard to gender implications" (West & Zimmerman, 1987, p. 142). The presentation of self through the cultural norms of linguistic discourses and forms of dress reflects the adolescent's gendered agency—the capacity for action, the consciousness and action itself (Mahmood, 2001).

The *body* is represented in the girls' experiences of how they visually and physically re-present themselves in person and in virtual spaces. Clothing choice and fit, and body-type and body-image can sometimes signal the adolescents' outsider position and non-member identity. Based on her interview responses, Sade is positioned as outsider. More so, she is a female who does not dress the way a female is expected to dress. According to Stritikus and Nguyen (2007), immigration is a gendered process with males and females being treated differently by their host society which leads to different patterns of social interaction and participation in the new host society and in transnational spaces. Thus, Sade reads the ways in which she is positioned by her peers and re-positions herself in a positive way even though it may conflict with her personal and family values ("The girls at school were totally different. They were into boys and stuff and I wasn't").

How the physical body is presented in the physical space shapes the ways in which the girls are received and identified. Their bodies also suggest normative behaviors around interests in the opposite sex. Stritikus and Nguyen (2007) indicated that as immigrant girls incorporate aspects of American cultural norms and reposition their gender identity, they often acquire higher social status and power. Labels and the physical representation of such labels of "female" and "girl/young woman" become identity markers; social networking sites and links to online shopping websites reinforce ascribed gender identities. The same could be said for Sade, who, by adopting cultural norms around dressing and the body, is better able to negotiate social networks at school. More so, the power this affords her is taken up in her digital networks where Sade now presents herself as promoting and embracing the norms, discourses, and practices related to dress, clothing and the body. Note that in Figure 7.1, Sade's Facebook home page signals her interest in clothing and with it, a particular level of taste and social class (e.g. Nordstrom is an upscale department store)—hence her "preppy-ish" dress/body image. The girls' interactions and online group membership reflect their nuanced understanding that negotiating the social contexts and group memberships within their adopted home requires attention to and conformity with the politics of re-production of the body and gender identity markers.

---

facebook

Sade

Sex: Female

Current City: Arima, GA

Relationship Status: Single

Me: Likes to travel, experience new things, new people, meet new people. Likes to shop. Listen to music. Independent.

ACCEPT DIFFERENCES BE KIND COUNT YOUR BLESSINGS DREAM EXPRESS THANKS

Pages: AmericanEagleOutfitters www.ae.com; Nordstrom.com
http://shop.pacsun.com/girls/; Fotographix; Christian/Rock

FIGURE 7.1 Sade's Facebook Homepage

Advocating for Self and Others

While the body (and the physical presentation of self) offers one way in which the young women position themselves, the online forum is also used as an advocacy site. Kai is ever aware of how her "difference" as newcomer/immigrant silenced her voice in her new/adopted home. She says:

> these girls—I remember—they called me some name. I don't remember what it was, but I hadn't heard it before. And, they like—they tried to . . . they tried to like, argue with me and all that kind of stuff. And, I just thought it was so bizarre like these girls would like, try and pick a fight with me. It's 'cause I'm new, and I really—I don't talk like them.
>
> I guess they had different priorities than me.
>
> *(Kai)*

In a later interview, Kai goes on to make a connection between her own silencing and her struggle for voice, and the main character in the novel *Speak*, with whom she identifies:

> Well, in Speak, it was about her finding her voice and just being able to speak up for herself. It's her first year in ninth grade and she had a rough summer, and it's basically just her trying to find herself.
>
> *(Kai)*

Borne out of this, perceived silencing, Kai used her digital literacies to find her voice and promote authentic dialogue for diverse youth, and around the topic of diversity. "So, I remember my group had to do diversity for the first semester, and we had to make a whole lesson plan, and we'd go teach it to them. And, that was really fulfilling." As seen in Figure 7.2, Kai's blog, *The Voice* creates a forum for "teens from diverse backgrounds develop skills to express themselves effectively and build a strong community." In so doing, Kai strategically creates a space for herself and others to participate in and create a community of voices online similar to her work in current event club and projects at school. Kai's efforts to find her voice expand into her virtual communities and networks.

One might argue that, perhaps, Kai's focus on having the voice of the "Other" be heard, may also restrict the mainstream or status quo. Yet, the very mode that she uses—a blog—though published and managed by her, opens discussion, dialogue, responses, and comments to everyone, and suggests that Kai is in fact open to dialogue, interactivity and to a multiple "world" views, relationships, and audience. The online forum facilitates such dialogue and local-global audience and issues. I would argue that her power and agency lies in their openness to engage in dialogue and position her as advocate for herself and others. Black Diaspora theorists (Gordon, 2000) contend that Africans and their descendants across the world use writing as a form of resistance and power. Here, Kai's decision to write, write online, and open the dialogue to online worlds suggests her awareness of the power of the word—her word—to reshape thinking and ideas in the world.

---

facebook

Kai

Sex: Female

Current City: Arima, GA

Relationship Status: Single

Interested In: Men

Me: there are too many things that i haven't done yet; too many sunsets i haven't seen
i can't waste the day wishing it'd slow down; i've been given this one world
i won't worry it away or lose sight of the good life;

Vexation of spirit is a waste of time. verbal conflict, a waste of word. physical conflict, a waste of flesh

Pages: *Voice:* Teens from diverse backgrounds develop skills to express themselves effectively and build a strong community.

The Beat is a forum that allows students to display their artwork, stories, commentaries, and poems online during the year.

FIGURE 7.2 Kai's Facebook Homepage

Contextualizing Language of Identity

> I mean, it doesn't really matter if you're Black, White, Chinese, Indian. You're still a person. It depends on your personality. And, I like people who are open-minded. I mean, to look beyond just color or looks. Look into somebody's personality as opposed to just judging them by what you see.
>
> *(Sade)*

The girls' ethnic identities were tied to language. In the case of Sade, she was conscious that *how* language is framed and ethnic/racial labels assigned or ascribed impact her participation in her adopted Home and communities. Bound up in these identity labels around race and ethnicity are the normative, denotative, connotative, and performative values and meanings. Ethnic/racial labels become a form of control and regulation of thought and action through a "standard" or normative way of reading the word and the world (Fanon, 1967; Freire, 1987). For Kai, dominant and authoritative discourses (Bakhtin, 1981) around race (in this case, African American identity label) confined her to a specific identity group, and denied her cosmopolitan identity. Bakhtin would argue that individuals are always engaging in dialogue with the authoritative discourse (homogeneous ideologies, actions, and values) and their internally persuasive discourse (personal experiences and views that may differ from and/or align with dominant discourse). In the case of Kai, the dominant socializing power of language around race and racial/ethnic categorizations regulates how she self-identifies.

> It's like, this curiosity about your race. I'm kind of to the point where if people ask me about my race, I'm just like, "human race." Seriously. Like, I had to fill out this mentoring program paper and you had to write what your race was and I wrote "human race." And, I'm sure that makes them mad.
>
> *(Kai)*

Kai's attempts to disrupt, challenge and resist the normative discourses and binaries around race, ethnicity, and national identity in school suggest her awareness of the power of language to construct identity. For migrant youth, language and identity labels signal membership and act as an identifier. Through language, identity shifts in context. Awareness of the power of language allows immigrant youth to access multiple affinity and identity groups.

Girls in Digital Worlds

Like many immigrant students/youth, social networks, digital literacy, and technology become identity markers (Lam & Rosario-Ramos, 2009; Guzzetti & Gamboa, 2004; McLean, 2010) signaling not only the young person's multimodal literacies but also their interconnection with the various communities to which they belong. Social networks and digital modes and spaces facilitated identity-construction by providing a forum for each young person to express her voice. The Facebook pages/sites offer insights into how they have each taken up their private experiences as immigrants and used them to purposefully help publicly position themselves in the world and to the world. Within their virtual spaces each is able to actively define herself in a way that advocates and challenges labels and stereotypes.

The adolescents' use of social networking sites such as Facebook represented the dynamic intersection of their global and local identities and contexts. The Internet social networks allowed both adolescents to move within and across multiple geographic and social spaces, but also to exercise some agency over the re-presentation of their identities. Digital literacies became the multimodal approach through which the girls resisted and re-presented traditional definitions of who they were as girls, racial/ethnic, and immigrants. Digital practices acted as a common *lingua franca* that made explicit their racial, ethnic and gendered identities and served to connect the girls globally and locally.

Implications for Literacy Teaching and Research

This study of immigrant girls' online literacy practices suggests the inter-connectedness of place, space, literacy, and the complex ways in which gender is represented and played out in online/digital literacy practices. The two adolescents' sense of selves as students were closely connected with their identities as female, immigrants and multiliterate beings. Stritikus and Nguyen (2007) state that gendered analyses of immigrant student adjustment offer a nuanced understanding of how gender shapes immigrant identity and adjustment. Awareness may mean a broadening of the purposes for which young persons use online texts, and more significantly, exploring with students the ways in which digital literacies may be used to connect, value, and re-present ethnic and gendered identities.

Teachers today face classrooms with diverse student populations and are expected to be culturally sensitive and to have skills for teaching a wide range of students (Ladson-Billings, 1995; Gay, 2000). Structuring classrooms in ways that facilitate interactions *across differences* supports the increased heterogeneity of schools (Sapon-Shevin, 1999). In-depth understanding of learners' identities requires capturing the process by which individuals—and communities—come to think of themselves, are framed by others, and are integrated into their local communities (Brayboy & Maughan, 2009). From a critical literacy perspective, this under-standing requires having the voices and experiences of the "other" and integrating them into educational processes, creating a fresh vantage point from which to analyze and understand immigrant learners within contemporary host classroom (Battiste, 2002).

Approaches to Practice

What might this contemporary host classroom look like? Pedagogical practice that honors diversity of immigrant learners takes a local/global approach to learning and teaching. It is characterized by an emphasis on choice and variety in the (1) content (2) con(text) and (3) multimedia.

Content

The classroom exposes students to a variety of literature that moves beyond the canon and classic literature. For example, teachers and media centers/libraries should offer a range of cosmopolitan and multicultural literature in the classroom that includes young adult literature. By approaching choice in terms of the genres, setting, characters and authors' gender/ethnic/racial identities, cultural practices, themes and issues, language style, etc., students are more likely to become engaged when they can "see" themselves in these texts.

Con(text)

Classroom activities and assignments can draw directly on students' backgrounds and experiences through activities that critique and critically look at representations of individuals and groups in the media (newspapers, television, movies, and advertisements). As an ongoing activity, students analyze, provide commentaries, and share their views on the various ways in which different social and identity groups are positioned and represented. By creating an environment that supports dialogue, and values students' perspectives and experiences, the classroom becomes a place that nurtures students' voice.

Multimedia

Language and literacy must draw on learners' digital and multimodal literacies. One such approach is through writing using digital and technological genres (e.g. blogs, podcasts, movies, digital stories, and zines). Learners can be provided opportunities to engage with classroom content using modes such as visuals, sounds, animation, interactivity, etc. to express themselves. For example, the character sketch is presented as a Facebook homepage, the historical essay is done in the form of a short documentary film, and students' blogs address their views on current affairs. The flexibility of modes, audience, writing styles/formats, etc. take into account students' various learning styles, interests, and literacy practices.

My position in this chapter is based on the view that, like policymakers, administrators, and educators, students are also conscious and agentive actors in their learning-teaching process. If schooling is to effectively provide equal educational opportunities to a culturally and literacy diverse population, then there needs to be greater opportunity for the voice of all learners to directly inform understanding.

References

Bakhtin, M.M. (1981). *Dialogic imagination: Four essays by M.M. Bakhtin* (C. Emerson & M. Holquist, Trans.; M. Holquist, Ed.). Austin: University of Texas Press.

Battiste, M. (2002). *Indigenous knowledge and pedagogy in first nations education: A literature review with recommendations.* Ottawa: Indian and Northern Affairs Canada.

Brayboy, B. & Maughan, E. (2009). Indigenous knowledge and the story of the bean. *Harvard Educational Review* 79(1), 1–21.

Comber, B. & Kamler, B. (1997). Critical literacies: Politicising the language classroom. *Interpretations*, 1–21.

Fanon, F. (1967). *Black skin, white masks* (C.L. Markmann, Trans.). New York: Grove Press.

Freire, P. (1987). *Literacy: Reading the word and the world.* South Hadley, MA: Bergin & Garvey.

Freire, P. & Macedo, D. (1995). A dialogue: Culture, language and race. *Harvard Educational Review,* 65(3), 377–402.

Gay, G. (2000). *Culturally responsive teaching: Theory, research, and practice.* New York: Teachers College Press.

Gee, J. (1999). *Social linguistics and literacies: Ideology in discourses.* London: Taylor & Francis.

Gordan, L.R. (2000). Existential Africana: Understanding Africana existential thought. New York: Routledge.

Guzzetti, B. & Gamboa, M. (2004). Zines for social justice: Adolescent girls writing on their own. *Reading Research Quarterly, 39*, 408–436.

Holland, D., Lachicotte, W., Skinner, D., & Cain, C. (1998). *Identity and agency in cultural worlds.* Cambridge, MA: Harvard University Press.

Ladson-Billings, G. (1995). But that's just good teaching! The case for culturally relevant pedagogy. *Theory Into Practice, 34*(3), 159–165.

Lam, E. & Rosario-Ramos, E. (2009). Multilingual literacies in transnational digitally mediated contexts: An exploratory study of immigrant teens in the United States. *Language and Education, 23*(2), 171–190.

Luke, A. (2004). On the material consequences of literacy. *Language and Education, 18*(4), 331–335.

Mahmood, S. (2001). Feminist theory, embodiment and the docile agent: Some reflections on the Egyptian Islamic revival. *Cultural Anthropology, 16*(2), 202–236.

McLean, C. (2010). A space called Home: An immigrant adolescent's literacy practices. *Journal of Adolescent and Adult Literacy. 54*(1), 13–22.

Miles, M.B. & Huberman, A.M. (1994). *Qualitative data analysis: A sourcebook of new methods.* Newbury Park, CA: Sage.

Morrell, E. (2004). Linking literacy and popular culture: Finding connections for lifelong learning. Norwood, MA: Christopher-Gordon Publishers:

Ryan, G. & Bernard, H.R. (2003). Techniques for identifying themes. *Field Methods, 15*(1), 85–109.

Sapon-Shevin, M. (1999). *Because we can change the world: A practical guide to building cooperative, inclusive classroom communities.* Boston: Allyn & Bacon.

Stritikus, T. & Nguyen, D. (2007). Strategic transformation: Cultural and gender identity negotiation in first generation Vietnamese youth. *American Educational Research Journal, 44*(4), 853–895.

West, C. & Zimmerman, D.H. (1987). Doing Gender. *Gender and Society,* 1(2), 125–151.

Williams, B.T. (2007). Girl power in a digital world: Considering the complexity of gender, literacy, and technology *Journal of Adolescent and Adult Literacy, 50*(4), 300–307.

8

ENTREPRENEURSHIP EDUCATION AND GENDERED DISCURSIVE PRACTICES

Donna E. Alvermann

Several bloggers whom I follow are increasingly focused on entrepreneurship education. For example, Julie Silard Kantor, Executive Director Network for Teaching Entrepreneurship (NFTE), had this to say about a pedagogy aimed at developing young people's entrepreneurial interests: "If done right, [it] impacts students' basic academic and life skills through a hands-on program and curriculum (think Mini MBA) that enlivens math, reading and writing, and develops skills in critical thinking, teamwork, communication and decision-making" (Kantor, 2012, 1). What this blogger leaves unsaid, however, is the significance of the interface between entrepreneurship education and young people's gendered discursive practices. Knowledge of that interface is central to any study of what youth take from their everyday world and apply to school-related learning. It is also central to the purpose of this chapter.

Here I draw from an eight-month study of five high school students' uses of web-based multimodal texts and social networking sites to carry out personal and academic agendas that they set for themselves (Alvermann et al., 2012). Specifically, I focus on Sandy (her self-chosen pseudonym), an African American tenth grader who was enrolled in a business education track that included courses on Business Law, Algebra I, Economics, and Business Processing. The Business Processing class provided the entrepreneurship assignment that is analyzed here in relation to Sandy's gendered discursive practices. Before moving into a discussion of that analysis, however, it is important to situate Sandy's goal of designing an online clothing store which she believed would simultaneously satisfy her Business Processing teacher's entrepreneurship assignment and her own personal interest in clothes that allow her to identify, in her words, "as a plain, simple, and sexy dresser."

A Global Curriculum for a Young Cyberflâneur

Young people today are growing up in an era in which information and communication technologies (ICTs) make it possible to participate in vast mediascapes of images and sounds that defy national boundaries for those who have access to reliable and high-speed Internet connections. Such access was not a part of Sandy's life until she volunteered to be one of five participants in a study funded by the Robert Bowne Foundation (Alvermann et al., 2012) that provided students with wireless connections and laptop computers which were theirs to keep in exchange for serving as co-researchers on the project.

Sandy's aesthetic sense of what she liked in clothes and the many hours she spent surfing websites for ideas on merchandising and how to stock her virtual clothing store reminded me of the young cyberflâneur that Kenway and Bullen (2008) described in their chapter on helping young people "see the downside of media-consumer culture, the contradictory tensions within the libidinal economy, without destroying their pleasures in it" (p. 22). The term "cyberflâneur" builds on an earlier understanding of *flâneur*—a somewhat dapper male figure who appeared in mid-nineteenth-century literature—a man who strolled city streets to observe urban life, a window shopper, of sorts (see Wikipedia, http://en.wikipedia.org/wiki/Flaneur). Noting the datedness of the term *flâneur* and its potential to stir controversy among feminists, Kenway and Bullen were quick to point out the following qualifications, which are still partial in scope:

> Today the object of the young cyberflâneur's inquiry is the global cultural economy and he or she is not limited by territoriality or time . . . [Moreover] the use of technology radically alters, if not obliterates, the relevance of the gendered body. Like cinema before it, ICTs permit a form of virtual flânerie that is available to women and girls.
>
> *(Kenway & Bullen, 2008, p. 24)*

Although a flâneur was conceived originally as "a solitary onlooker"—someone who stood outside or apart from the production phase of entrepreneurship (Wilson, 1992, p. 95)—this is no longer the case. The young cyberflâneur of today who has access to the Internet can use it as a tool for looking beyond the glitz of a global consumer culture to discover connections between, say, an upscale clothing website and instances of animal cruelty. Activist videos can also function as connectors, especially if they parody commercialization and consumer behaviors (e.g., "Let's Go Spend Some Money" http://www.adbusters.org/abtv/lets_go_spend_some_money.html). Such videos are often playfully critical and not intended to squelch the pleasures that someone like Sandy might bring to an assignment in entrepreneurship education.

Gendered Discursive Practices

To explore the frequently overlooked interface between entrepreneurship education and young people's gendered discursive practices, I chose a feminist poststructuralist lens through which to interpret the writings of twentieth-century French philosopher and historian Michel Foucault. According to Foucault (1990 [1978]), "Discourse transmits and produces power; it reinforces it, but also undermines and exposes it, renders it fragile and makes it possible to thwart it" (p. 101). Poststructuralist feminists who took up Foucault's notion of discourse (e.g., Brodkey, 1992; Butler, 1990; Weedon, 1997) have studied the ways in which gendered discourse governs how individuals think, feel, and act. Of particular relevance to Sandy's case is Weedon's (1997) interpretation of Foucault—one that contextualizes the authenticity of individual experiences. In Weedon's words:

> Although the subject in poststructuralism is socially constructed in discursive practices, she nonetheless exists as a thinking, feeling subject and social agent, capable of resistance . . . [with the ability to] reflect upon the discursive relations which constitute her and the society in which she lives . . . [and] to choose from the options available.
>
> *(Weedon, 1997, p. 121)*

Situating herself as a feminist poststructuralist, Fine (1992) brought insights from her work as a social psychologist to bear on breaking silences around taken-for-granted power inequities and vested interests in education. Although Fine's work is not focused specifically on the intersection of entrepreneurship education and gendered discursive practices, it seemingly could support a call for questioning certain assumptions about websites that display what Sandy describes as "plain, simple, and sexy" clothing.

To me, such a call requires a methodology that permits comparing and contrasting websites for what Stone and Veth (2008) described as the cultural modeling of "opposites," or in their words, "how the sites framed members of the opposite sex" (p. 31). In choosing to analyze the three websites that Sandy visited most frequently in her bid to locate clothing suitable for the virtual store she was designing in response to a Business Processing class assignment, I expanded Stone and Veth's (2008) methodology. Specifically, I needed a methodology that would take into account gendered discursive practices that embrace diversity as a way of complicating the normalized male/female binary. Websites that problematized identity categories associated with certain clothing styles (e.g., men's and women's outerwear), I reasoned, would give me insight into Sandy's understanding of the three criteria—"plain, simple, and sexy"—that she imposed on the class assignment.

Data Sources and Procedures for Analyzing Websites

This case study's primary data sources included Sandy's weekly logs of the websites that she had visited on a daily basis from Saturday through Friday for eight months. In my role as researcher, I sat side by side with her as she talked me through her logs and showed me the websites on her laptop computer that aligned with the log's entries. As Sandy talked, I audio-recorded our conversations about the sites and the various practices in which she engaged. I also transcribed data from three informal interviews with her and requested permission to analyze various artifacts (e.g., a PowerPoint of the clothing she found plain, simple, and sexy). All data collection took place for one hour on Saturday mornings while Sandy was enrolled in an academic support program called the Empowered Youth Program (EYP). Sponsored by the counseling education department at my university, the EYP offered opportunities for young men and women from local secondary schools to practice leadership and academic skills.

Following Stone and Veth (2008), I analyzed each of the three clothing websites that Sandy visited most frequently for cultural models of gender (Gee, 1999). According to Gee, cultural models "are our 'first thoughts' or taken-for-granted assumptions about what is 'typical' or 'normal'" (p. 59). Unfortunately, as Gee pointed out, "Cultural models often involve us in exclusions that . . . set up [criteria for] what count as central, typical cases, and what count as marginal, non-typical cases" (p. 59). When this occurs, cultural models can be harmful, especially if they result in unfair, dismissive, or derogatory assumptions about other people. In analyzing the three clothing websites for cultural models of gender, I asked how each one's design and content characterized the "opposite" sex. The term "opposite" is enclosed within quotation marks to indicate my refusal to essentialize (or solidify in stone) what it means to be male, female, lesbian, gay, bisexual, or transgender people.

Descriptions of the three websites are included next for the purpose of contextualizing my interpretation of what each site likely contributed to the gendered discursive practices that Sandy brought to the entrepreneurship assignment. In the second section—the cultural modeling of gender on clothing websites—I speculatively allude to why Sandy may have had few opportunities to question the assumptions that underlie the male/female binary, especially in regard to brand name clothing. Finally, I draw implications for literacy instruction at the point where entrepreneurship education interfaces with gendered discursive practices—or at least those gendered practices as represented in Sandy's Business Processing project.

Descriptions of Three Clothing Websites

A pre-analysis of each of the three clothing websites that Sandy visited most frequently—Baby Phat (http://www.babyphat.com/shop.php), Rocawear (http://www.Rocawear.com), and Apple Bottoms (http://www.applebottom.com/)—

indicated that none of these websites complicated the normalized male/female binary. Thus, in the descriptions that follow, my analyses are limited to women's and men's wear as pictured separately on the websites that Sandy visited.

Baby Phat

Babyphat.com is the brand name for an urban fashion line that includes clothing, footwear, handbags, accessories for phones, jewelry, and fragrances for women and girls. Its logo, symbolized by a sleek pink cat, contains the words "From the runway to the pavement." According to the company's overview on its Facebook page, "Baby Phat first hit the scene when tiny tees with the clever name Baby Phat (an acronym for 'pretty, hot and tempting') were produced to electrify a Phat Farm runway show" (https://www.facebook.com/BabyPhatFashions/info).

Phat Farm, Baby Phat's corporate sibling, reflects "men's contemporary American culture, mixing the urban aesthetics of the streets and the preppy culture of the Ivy League . . . for example, argyle sweaters are paired with baggy jeans and crisp white sneakers" (http://en.wikipedia.org/wiki/Phat_farm). In the company's overview on its Facebook page, Phat Farm is described as a classic collection "carved out of the hearts and souls of hip hop enthusiasts . . . whose apparel needs . . . [fit] a lifestyle and attitudes of young men who aspire to live well and have an affinity for style" (https://www.facebook.com/OfficialPhatFarm/info/). Its brand DNA is captured in these words: "Classic with a twist."

When I was looking for examples of cultural modeling of "opposites" on Baby Phat's and Phat Farm's websites, they were easy to come by. For example, the tennis shoes and sneakers on both of these websites differed according to what one might predict for an uncomplicated category: Baby Phat's styling was more decorative and came in pastel colors, whereas Phat Farm's styling was more traditional and came in classic earth tones. Both sites' outerwear for women and men aligned well with Sandy's preferences for the *plain* and *simple*. They differed only on her third criterion. The word "sexy," which appeared 16 times on Baby Phat's website, referred exclusively to female models' cropped jeans (www.baby phat.com/nshop/product.php?page=1&view=keyword&keywords=sexy) and not the tiny tees that had reputedly electrified Phat Farm's runway. Although more difficult to track down, the word "sexy" appeared on a Phat Farm websites that featured pimp cups (http://www.icedoutgear.com/phat-farm.php).

Rocawear

According to the company's overview, Rocawear.com sets the standard that defines today's young hip consumers and their lifestyle in general. Launched by Shawn "Jay-Z" Carter and Damon Dash, Rocawear apparel claims it represents a borderless, global lifestyle by appealing to street savvy consumers. With revenues reaching $700 million in fiscal year 2007, Rocawear expanded its brand to include socks, and sandals, leather, suede and fur outerwear, handbags, headwear, jewelry, and belts. From references provided on Wikipedia.org, it appears that allegations were made in 2007 of tanuki fur (from the raccoon dog that is native to eastern Asia) being used in jackets. At that point in time, decisions were made by the company to pull the jackets from all department stores and to remove them from Rocawear's official website (http://en.wikipedia.org/wiki/Rocawear).

Both men's and women's clothing are displayed on Rocawear.com (unlike Baby Phat and Phat Farm, which, while corporate siblings, maintain separate websites and Facebook pages). The clothing for both men and women (e.g., jean styles) are similar at Rocawear. In this instance, the cultural modeling of "opposites" is difficult if not impossible to detect. Two of Sandy's three inclusion criteria for her imaginary store (*plain* and *simple*) are met on Rocawear's website. The third criterion, *sexy* is not met for the most part. For example, the term "sexy" is associated with only five items on Rocawear.com: (a) a woman's tee that sells for $14.97; (b) a necklace with the letters s-e-x-y on the pendant for $9.97; (c) a pair of women's skinny jeans for $58.98; (d) a pair of men's black Bermuda shorts for $19.97; and (e) a woman's zippered tricot jacket for $49.99 (http://www.roca wear.com/productsearch/q/sexy/none/rank).

Apple Bottoms

This website's motto—"A woman should not try to fit the clothes, the clothes should fit the woman"—addressed all three of Sandy's requirements (*plain, simple, and sexy*). With 73 items on its website sporting the label "sexy" in the women's clothing line and zero items carrying that same label in the men's line, Apple Bottoms is definitely the poster child website for the cultural modeling of "opposites." The website also points to the cultural modeling of opposites in men's and women's clothing choices, the poses models choose, and other more subtle nuances (e.g., the object of a model's gaze, the size of the model, and the brightness or drabness of colors).

Touted as a fashion and lifestyle brand that rap artist Nelly helped to launch in 2003, Wikipedia lists this for the company's tagline: "Apples come in all shapes and sizes" (http://en.wikipedia.org/wiki/Apple_bottom). Apple Bottoms signifies "a woman whose curvaceous figure is revealed by her tight-fitting jeans, resembling the shape of an apple" (http://en.wikipedia.org/wiki/Apple_bottom). It also alludes to differences in some women's body types, such as a pear-shaped vs. an hourglass figure. Initially, Apple Bottoms carried a denim label as its brand; however, the company has since expanded to include other women's and girls' clothing, shoes, bags, perfume, and accessories. A brand referenced in several hip hop songs, including two by Nelly, Apple Bottoms gained added visibility when Oprah Winfrey wore a pair of Apple Bottoms Jeans on her television show and subsequently added that brand to her annual list of Oprah's favorite things.

Cultural Modeling of Gender on Clothing Websites

It might be argued that Sandy was a cyberflâneur in her quest for clothing that satisfied her three criteria; nonetheless, she certainly exercised her own judgment, made up her own mind as to what to include or exclude, and generally demonstrated a flair for entrepreneurship. Seemingly somewhat aware of the gendered discursive practices that constituted her and the society in which she lived, Sandy told me in my interviews with her that she felt the Business Processing class had prepared her to choose wisely from the options available. To underscore her self-confidence, Sandy prepared a PowerPoint presentation in which one of the slides emphasized that her store could easily overcome its competition. In Sandy's words:

- Plain, Simple, & Sexy is a store that will keep it basic and uncomplicated but will also preserve your sexy.
- With low prices and the most updated fashions we overcome the competition that we once had.
- Walking into our store you shall fill [sic] a warm welcome and assurance that will keep you coming back.

Although Rocawear, one of the clothing websites that Sandy visited, seemed well positioned to interrupt certain gendered discursive practices in that it did not differentiate clothing on the basis of the male/female binary, the others (Baby Phat/Phat Farm and Apple Bottoms) fell neatly in line with the cultural modeling of "opposites"—even to the point of relying on well-known celebrities to advertise their brand by wearing it. Such validation by branding is likely to have lessened any chance of Sandy's questioning the assumptions underlying the cultural modeling of "opposites." In similar manner, it is likely Sandy took from the entrepreneurship project little information that might prompt her to complicate the male/female binary at a future point in time. With their identity categories well hardened, Baby Phat/Phat Farm and Apple Bottoms played directly to the gendered discursive practices that Sandy is likely to have brought with her to the entrepreneurship project.

Implications for Literacy Instruction

Sandy had the fewest entries in her weekly logs of all the participants in the larger study despite the fact she used the Internet more than the other students to research information needed for school-related assignments, such as the one just described. In interviews with me, Sandy divulged that she did not like to read for the purpose of writing school-related papers because she found it difficult to plod through an entire book page after page. She reiterated on several occasions that she much preferred to skim a text to find relevant information—a likely factor in her interest in browsing the Internet for clothes that fit her three criteria.

Perhaps at most, this mini-study of the interface between entrepreneurship education and gendered discursive practices has pointed out the necessity of considering the underlying assumptions of both factors when designing pedagogies aimed at developing young people's entrepreneurial interests. In terms of entrepreneurship education, there is the tendency to assume that classes such as Business Processing have little or no need to connect their curricula to issues of gendered cultural modeling. In like manner, gendered discursive practices are seldom topics of discussion in high school subjects that make up the business education curriculum.

This absence of overlap has implications for literacy instruction. First and foremost, this absence points to a pedagogical void in bridging content and process, an issue that has plagued secondary literacy instruction for decades. However, with the rollout of the Common Core State Standards in most school districts across the United States in 2012–2013, teachers are increasingly exposed to ways of integrating literacy instruction with subject matter learning. What better time than now to develop an awareness of how students' gendered discursive practices are brought uncritically into entrepreneurship education projects, such as Sandy's, and then reified ever more deeply by the very technology that purports to prepare students to be college and career ready.

With a slight fine-tuning of the virtual store project in which Sandy so willingly engaged, it might be possible to introduce activities in which students question the underlying assumptions of gendered cultural modeling. What, for example, does the very name Apple Bottoms inscribe in one's memory? Whose image is enhanced? Whose is lowered, and with what consequences? Discussions that fold critical thinking and reading into subject matter learning can also elicit writing and other modes of communicating (imagery, sound, performance) about gendered discursive practices that need overturning and then renewing.

References

Alvermann, D.E., Marshall, J.D., McLean, C.A., Huddleston, A.P., Joaquin, J., & Bishop, J. (2012). Adolescents' web-based literacies, identity construction, and skill development. *Literacy Research and Instruction, 51*, 1–17.

Brodkey, L. (1992). Articulating poststructural theory in research on literacy. In R. Beach, M.L. Kamil, & T. Shanahan (Eds.), *Multidisciplinary perspectives on literacy research* (pp. 293–318). Urbana, IL: National Conference on Research in English and National Council of Teachers of English.

Butler, J.P. (1990). *Gender trouble: Feminism and the subversion of identity.* New York: Routledge.

Fine, M. (1992). *Disruptive voices: The possibilities of feminist research.* Ann Arbor, MI: University of Michigan Press.

Foucault, M. (1990). *The history of sexuality: Vol.I, An introduction* (R. Hurley, Trans.). New York, NY: Vintage. (Original work published 1978).

Gee, J.P. (1999). *An introduction to discourse analysis: Theory and method.* London: Routledge.

Kantor, J.S. (2012). Youth entrepreneurship: A mission that has met its time. Retrieved March 28, 2012, from http://youthentrepreneurshiplady.wordpress.com/category/julie-silard-kantor/

Kenway, J. & Bullen, E. (2008). The global corporate curriculum and the young cyberflâneur as global citizen. In N. Dolby & F. Rizvi (Eds.), *Youth moves: Identities and education in global perspective* (pp. 17–31). New York: Routledge.

Stone, J.C. & Veth, E.S. (2008). Rethinking the new literatures of childhood: Cultural models of gender in popular websites. *Journal of Language and Literacy Education* [Online], *4*(2), 21–39. Retrieved March 30, 2012, from http://www.coe.uga.edu/jolle/2008/rethinking.pdf

Weedon, C. (1997). *Feminist practice and poststructuralist theory* (2nd ed.). Oxford: Blackwell.

Wilson, E. (1992). The invisible flâneur. *New Left Review, 191,* 90–110.

9

A CAUTIONARY TALE

Online School Book Clubs are No Panacea for African American Adolescent Females' Coming to Voice

Benita R. Dillard

In the early 1980s, Elsie Smith wrote an article tracing the educational, career, and psychological development of the Black adolescent female. Research in the 1990s (Fordham, 1993; Horvat & Antonio, 1999) and beyond (Eggleston & Miranda, 2009; Evans-Winters, 2005; Muhammad & Dixson, 2008) highlighted an unjust educational system that reflects "ongoing, pervasive silencing as well as curtailed access to literacy learning for social, economic, and personal empowerment" (Wissman, 2007–2008, p. 341). The results of these studies indicated that African American girls' educational experiences comprised of racism, alienation, and isolation. Traditional forms of literacy education still required African American adolescent females to remain silent and invisible. In the 21st century, they continue to confront an academic literary canon and a classroom pedagogy that require immersing themselves in the "sedentary activities of reading, writing, and speaking in a way that is structured by certain racist, gender, and class privileges" (Henry, 2005, pp. 72–73).

The following excerpts from one-on-one chat-room interviews I had with African American adolescent females enrolled in a public charter, online high school illustrate this point. In an interview with Isabella (pseudonyms are used for all the girls), a sophomore, she revealed, "I don't remember reading any books by African American females." Haunted by these words I felt, as a Black female, educator, and researcher, it was my moral responsibility to provide opportunities for them to read about and discuss their experiences, resist, and even construct cultural meanings found in young adult fiction written by African American female authors. Therefore, this qualitative research offered Isabella, Bianca, and Esperanza an opportunity to use three online spaces: (1) single-gendered chat-room group discussions, (2) emails, and (3) VoiceThreads to discuss their lived experiences. The online spaces provided anonymity, an opportunity for relationships to be established, and participation in "a range of information activities and learning experiences" (Lankshear et al., p. 160).

Findings: A Journey of Self-Discovery

This section examined the ways that Isabella, Bianca, and Esperanza's responses problematized the notion that online book clubs are neutral spaces, devoid of the power issues that operate in small group classroom discussions. For instance, Esperanza found the literature mirrored her experiences, while Bianca struggled to connect with protagonists and issues addressed in the literature.

The terms "African American" and "Black" are used in the findings and implication sections interchangeably. In this context, however, the term "African American" designates a shared ethnicity, while the term "Black" is broad enough to identify Isabella and Bianca who possessed visible characteristics ascribed to Black people while identifying as Biracial, Black, or African American (Henry, 1998a).

Isabella, Bianca, and Esperanza discussed four young adult novels written by African American female authors in the online spaces provided. The novels were: Sharon Flake's *The Skin I'm In* (1998), Jacqueline Woodson's *Hush* (2002), Sharon Draper's *Double Dutch* (2002), and Lori A. Williams's *When Kambia Elaine Flew in from Neptune* (2000). Flake illustrated through the protagonist Maleeka Madison how the social construct of skin color impacted a dark-skinned female's life. Woodson examined the protagonist Toswiah (Evie) as she searched for answers to define who she was while she and her family were in a Witness Protection Program. In Draper's novel, the characters lived double lives. Williams's novel addressed different types of pain that most African American females experienced.

Isabella

Isabella committed to this project despite the challenges she faced with getting other group members to read the novels. There were two different groups. One group met on Tuesday and the other met online on Thursday. Isabella participated in Thursday's group with Angel, Aurora, and Jade. Isabella was the only one from that group that logged on to all the chat-room group discussions. Isabella self-identified as a 15-year-old, Biracial female who embraced her African American heritage. In the chat-room group discussion on Flake's novel, Isabella shared, "I don't know anyone on my dad's side . . . My mom and dad divorced when I was 4 and then my dad died when I was 7." When asked to explain why she did not communicate with her father's side, she did not respond to the question. Instead, she revealed, "Most of my friends are White and the only family I know is White so it is kinda hard sometimes." Isabella struggled with the fact that "no one on my mother's side looked like me." In her grandmother's eyes, "I am not black at all." In fact, her grandmother prohibited her from braiding her hair because "She doesn't like my African American background." According to Isabella, her grand-mother showed favoritism toward the other grandchildren because they were White.

Isabella described in the first email interview that the atmosphere in the single-gendered book club was contentious at times. Yet, she claimed, "We understood each other most of the time. We had some moments where we didn't see eye to eye but it wasn't a big deal!" In addition, she noticed, "The other participants didn't finish the book before the discussion." Isabella declared, "I don't know how they expected to discuss the book if they didn't read it all." For Isabella, the anonymity in the online chat-room environment enabled her to feel comfortable expressing herself openly and freely. Yet, she felt the single-gendered book club could have been more valuable if her fellow participants had read the books.

Isabella found the novels taught her "about past experiences, and about the world outside my own." For example, Isabella did not know that "the darkness of skin color was an issue for some people." She believed it was important to address the issue of skin color and thought Flake did "a very good job addressing the issues because we all sometimes feel like outcast and want a place to belong." She mentioned feeling like an outcast when around her grandmother. Despite feeling like an outcast, she believed people saw her as someone that was shy but had hidden potential. She claimed, "My mom says people see me as a spiritual person." When asked how she saw herself, Isabella responded with, "I am Christian; I am bi-racial, I am a teenager; I am a student; I am an American; I can also be very rebellious. I am me."

Isabella considered Williams's novel her favorite. The issue that resonated with her the most was not "to judge someone for their looks." Isabella saw in the character Doo-Witty how "Everyone judged him and thought he was a big dummy." Isabella believed he was "far from a big dummy." In fact, Doo-Witty opened Isabella's eyes and allowed her to see that people, in particular her grandmother, were going to judge her regardless. Through Doo-Witty, she realized that it was time to stop blaming herself for her grandmother's unwillingness to accept the fact that being Black was part of her heritage. Isabella concluded in her VoiceThread, "I am happy with me; if someone isn't happy with me; then who needs them. I'm just me; take it or leave it."

In the beginning, Isabella could not recall reading any books written by African American female writers. In the end, she wrote, "Now I know of at least 4 amazing books written by extraordinary people; can't wait to read more by them." She attributed the safety in the online chat-room environment to anonymity. Because she could remain anonymous, she did not fear being judged. Isabella concluded that this study "warmed my heart" and "taught me that it was ok to talk about my thoughts and feelings."

Bianca

Bianca participated in Tuesday's group with Esperanza and Star. She participated in all the online chat-room group discussions. Bianca self-identified as a 17-year-old, Biracial female. Bianca's mother was Black, and her father was White. In the initial one-on-one chat-room interview, Bianca revealed that she thought the research study would be face-to-face. Because she thought it would be face-to-face, she feared that, "I was too fair-skinned to be considered 'right' for it." When asked to explain, she wrote, "I was concerned that if OTHER people could see me, would they wonder why she picked the whitest black girl to be a part of her study?" When asked if she struggled with her racial/ethnic identity, Bianca declared, "I am proud of who I am." She continued, "I have been given the greatest friends and family on earth. Because I am one of Jehovah's Witnesses, I have friends of all ages and races. I never think about what 'color' I am." She wrote, "I have never encountered stereotypes, primarily because of my religion, and I have been home-schooled all my life."

In the initial one-on-one chat-room interview, Bianca could not recall any African American female authors' names. In all our email interviews, Bianca stated that the online chat-room environment allowed her to see different perspectives. In the final email interview, Bianca shared that she felt uneasy when "we were discussing Kambia's abuse [in Flake's novel]." It was the graphic details the author used to describe Kambia's appearance after being molested that made Bianca feel uncomfortable. As a result, she did not "feel anything different reading books written by African American females." Bianca declared, "I don't really care who the author is or what color the main character is, so long as it's a good story." It became evident that Bianca was disappointed with the literature selection for this research.

In the final chat room group discussion on Williams's novel, Bianca described the novel as depressing. She wrote, "I mean we get enough bad things happening in real life. Why read about it when we can just turn on the news? I would not recommend this book to a friend because I didn't really like it." Bianca revealed in the final email interview that she would not recommend this book because she was "disgusted with the amount of depravity in it." Bianca rejected the issues discussed in this novel because it contradicted the teachings of her religion and her reading preference. When asked to explain, she used Tia's relationship with Doo-Witty. She stated, "I would never get involved with someone in that way unless I was married to that person." Bianca believed it was inappropriate for authors, in this case African American female authors, to write young adult literature that included graphic details such as sexual abuse. In the chat-room group discussion, Bianca reiterated that she did not like "to read depressing books" because "reading is my time to get away into a fantasy world. I like to completely go out into fiction. No realistic fiction stories here!"

Esperanza

In the initial one-on-one chat-room interview, Esperanza recalled bad experiences that clouded her perspective on Black people. She had Black peers call her "too White" and an "Oreo" cookie. According to Esperanza, Black peers often used these phrases to describe her because "I listened to metal and couldn't care less about rap." Adolescent Black males would not date Esperanza because "I'm Black." In Esperanza's case, adolescent Black males found the color of her skin too dark and less attractive, yet continued to stereotype her as acting "too White." These experiences contributed to her thinking negatively about Black people.

Nonetheless, Esperanza, 17 years old, committed to the entire research. She used the email interviews to disclose her thoughts and opinions on the online chat-room environment. In the first email interview, she revealed that it gave "Black girls a chance to express themselves and encourage one another." In the second email interview, she wrote the online chat-room environment helped "others anonymously express their feelings." In the third email interview, she wrote that the online chat-room "gave them a chance to talk and freely discuss" issues relevant to their lives. It became evident that the anonymity provided by the online chat-room enabled her to feel there was "No reason to hold back ideas or opinions." She used the email interviews to describe her experiences in the single-gendered book club. In the first email interview, she shared, "I didn't feel uncomfortable talking about race." She referred to the fact that, "Race is an open subject in my household." This single-gendered book club made her feel as though she was discussing race with a relative. She felt the online chat-room group discussions were very open, friendly, and understanding.

Esperanza commented in the email interviews that the novels addressed issues that most people are afraid to discuss openly. She believed the authors wrote the novels in a "classy way that won't step on anyone's toes." She expressed how much she appreciated the way author Sharon Flake addressed the issue of skin color in the Black community. As a darker skinned, adolescent, Black female, Esperanza shared in the chat-room group discussion that she never had a problem with being darker than the rest of her friends; the adolescent Black males had a problem with it. Esperanza believed, "The lighter you are, the closer you are to being accepted." For this reason, she appreciated the fact that Flake's novel addressed this issue because she felt "it's important that girls know that being black or dark isn't an ugly thing."

It became evident that Esperanza believed Black females needed to forge independent self-definitions to counter stereotypical images. In the final chat-room group discussion on Williams's novel, Esperanza shared that she thought the author portrayed Black females in stereotypical ways. When asked what she would change about the novel, she wrote, "I would change the way Black people are depicted in here." Esperanza believed Black people, in particular Black female writers, needed to stop perpetuating stereotypes. Esperanza wrote, "If we don't stop putting each other down, then who will?"

Overall, Esperanza considered the spaces to be safe for discourse. She attributed the safety in the online chat-room environment to its anonymity. She considered the single-gendered book club to be safe because the other group participants were always friendly and considerate. Likewise, she believed the novels offered a safe space for her to talk about issues that "most people are afraid to bring up." In sum, the spaces helped Esperanza "to see Black people in a more positive light" and "discuss issues that we face as Black people in our community in a very wholesome safe environment."

Implications for Literacy Education

While scholarship examining the literacy experiences of African American adolescent females is evident, progress overall has been quite limited. Most scholarship on African American adolescent girls' literacy experiences examined how they responded to African American contemporary young adult fiction (Brooks et al., 2008; Sutherland, 2005) or poetic work written by African American female poets (Wissman, 2007–2008). Wissman found "grounding literacy work within the literacy tradition of African-American women supported learning environments where literacy is enacted as a social practice, where inquiry is pursued, and where knowledge is constructed relationally" (p. 18). Wissman believed literacy work within this tradition provided opportunities for young Black females to come to voice. She found it difficult to articulate on paper what transpired in the classroom, yet Wissman described the experience as electricity filling the room. Brooks et al. (2008) used Sharon Flake's (1998) novel *The Skin I'm In*, believing it would offer opportunities for the voices of African American adolescent females, from working-class and middle-class families, to be heard. They believed African American girls gained self-affirmation from stories about trustworthy representations of African American female adolescents. Despite providing trustworthy depictions of African American girls, Brooks et al. found the participants revealed a more complicated and multifaceted nature of "reader-text identifications, partly because of the shifting identities" (p. 662). Underpinning the scholarship was the belief that the literacy tradition of African American female authors provided a safe space as described by Black feminist scholars for Black females to come to voice.

Findings in this research suggested that adolescent Black females reading contemporary realistic young adult fiction written by African American female writers was not always a safe space, as some Black feminist scholars described it (Collins, 1990). The findings revealed that race was more complex, and as a result, the exact match from literature to girls was not enough to meet their needs. As such, the implication drawn here is based on what the research did not say about the literacy education of African American adolescent females. Literacy education for adolescent Black girls should focus on adopting a critical literacy approach, moving them into a more deconstructive stance in regards to multicultural literature. According to Sturtevant and Moore (2009–2010), literacy education should think globally, encouraging our adolescents "to think beyond their own locales and develop understandings about people and issues" even in other parts of the world (p. 339).

Equally important, literacy education should consider locating alternative in-school spaces for adolescent Black females to come to voice. According to Scott (2004), the online chat-room provided Black girls with safe social experiences. Scharber et al. (2009) discovered online book clubs offered a forum that capitalized on adolescents' familiarity with computers and New Literacy practices while staying rooted in traditional practices. In other words, it effectively weaved together old and new literacy practices. Findings in this research revealed the anonymity in the online chat-room environment enabled some to feel safe because they did not have to worry about any form of accountability or assessment. The findings also revealed there was no certainty in the online chat-room environment. For this reason, literacy education should consider using other alternative spaces, such as VoiceThread. The findings suggested that African American adolescent females found VoiceThread to be a safe space to reject multicultural literature and speak openly about racism and its impact on their lives.

Literacy education should also consider what could go wrong in a single-gendered book club. Scharber, Melrose, and Wurl's (2009) research found girls were very active and enthusiastic to talk about books in a single-gendered online space because it provided a "safe, guided social experience" (p. 188). Findings in this research revealed group dynamics are unpredictable, and as a result, creating spaces exclusively for adolescent Black females to authentically learn about and express themselves in subjective ways might not be as safe as some researchers and theorists have argued (Collins, 1990; Henry, 1998b). Literacy education that envisions certain locations as safe spaces for African American adolescent females to discuss issues relevant to them must remember there is no monolithic Black female culture, so what worked for one group may not work for another. In sum, this chapter presents a cautionary tale; there is no panacea for African American adolescent females' coming to voice.

References

Brooks, W., Browne, S., & Hampton, G. (2008). "There ain't no accounting for what folks see in their own mirrors": Considering colorism within a Sharon Flake narrative. *Journal of Adolescent & Adult Literacy*, 660–669.

Collins, P.H. (1990). *Black feminist thought: Knowledge, consciousness, and the politics of empowerment*. Boston: Union Hyman.

Draper, S.M. (2002). *Double Dutch*. New York: Atheneum Books for Young Readers.

Eggleston, T. & Miranda, A.H. (2009). Black girls' voices: Exploring their lived experiences in a predominately white high school. *Race/ethnicity: Multidisciplinary Global Contexts*, 2, 259–285.

Evans-Winters, V.E. (2005). *Teaching Black girls: Resiliency in urban classrooms*. New York: Peter Lang.

Flake, S. (1998). *The skin I'm in*. New York: Jump at the Sun.

Fordham, S. (1993). Those loud Black girls: Black women, silence, and gender "passing" in the academy. *Anthropology & Education Quarterly, 24*, 3–32.

Henry, A. (1998a). Speaking up and speaking out: Examining voice in a reading/writing program with adolescent African Caribbean girls. *Journal of Literacy Research, 30*, 233–252.

Henry, A. (1998b). Invisible and womanish: Black girls negotiating their lives in an African-centered school in the USA. *Race, Ethnicity, and Education, 1*, 151–170.

Henry, A. (2005). Writing in the margins of classroom life: A teacher/researcher partnership using dialogue journals. In L. Pease-Alvarez, (Ed.) *Learning, teaching, and community: Contributions of situated and participatory approaches to educational innovation* (pp. 69–87). Mahweh, NJ: Lawrence Erlbaum Associates.

Horvat, E. & Antonio, A. (1999). Hey, those shoes are out of uniform: African American girls in an elite high school and the importance of habitus. *Anthropology & Education Quarterly, 30*, 317–342.

Lankshear, C., Peters, M., & Knobel, M. (1996). Critical pedagogy and cyberspace. In H. Giroux, C. Lankshear, P. McLaren, & M. Peters, *Counternarratives: Cultural studies and critical pedagogies in postmodern spaces* (pp. 149–188). New York: Routledge.

Muhammad, C.G. & Dixson, A.D. (2008). Black females in high school: A statistical educational profile. *Negro Education Review, 59*, 163–180.

Scharber, C.M., Melrose, A., & Wurl, J. (2009). Online book clubs for preteens and teens. *Library Review, 58*, 176–195.

Scott, K.A. (2004). African American–White Girls' Friendships. *Feminism & Psychology, 14*, 383–388.

Sturtevant, E.G. & Moore, D.W. (2009–2010). Understanding the local and global in adolescent literacy: An interview with Elizabeth G. Sturtevant. *Journal of Adolescent and Adult Literacy, 53*, 337–339.

Sutherland, L.M. (2005). Black adolescent girls' use of literacy practices to negotiate boundaries of ascribed identity. *Journal of Literacy Research*, 365–406.

Williams, L.A. (2000). *When Kambia Elaine flew in from Neptune*. New York: Simon & Schuster.

Wissman, K. (2007–2008). The beginning of a beloved community: Teaching and learning within the literacy tradition of African American women writers. *WILLA, 16*, 14–20.

Woodson, J. (2002). *Hush*. New York: Putnam.

10

GENDER, MULTIMODAL PRACTICES, AND GLOBAL CITIZENSHIP IN RURAL SETTINGS

Carla K. Meyer and Leslie Susan Cook

Advances in technology have further complicated traditional divisions among rural, suburban, and urban communities. Over the past decade, as technology has been eroding geographic boundaries, the concepts of global village and cottage communities have gained momentum (Graham & Marvin, 1996). Communication is no longer bound by time or place. Technologies allow us to simultaneously exchange information and ideas without travel (Valentine & Holloway, 2001). Not only do information communication technologies eliminate time/space barriers, they also provide new spaces for exchange to occur (Stone, 1992). As barriers of time and distance have faded, the concept of global citizenship, or cosmopolitanism, has grown. For many, the idea of a cosmopolitan citizen is attractive because it unites individuals to the idea of civil society (Arnot, 2009) or a community of humankind (Nussbaum, 2002). Still, boundaries exist.

Working at a Southeastern U.S. university nestled in the Blue Ridge Mountains of North Carolina, we recognized the barriers and breakthroughs resulting from urban/rural boundaries. The lives of rural youth have become part of our own. Our partnerships with rural schools and our work with teachers, assisting them in integrating and implementing multimodal composition pedagogical practices across the curriculum, served to increase our awareness of the circumstances in which rural youth participated in online global communities. This involvement with the local school systems has also made us aware of the disparities in access to and use of technology within neighboring school counties. Because of the limited access rural youth had to technology even in schools, we began to wonder what they were doing with technology outside school walls. The National Education Technology Plan (United States Department of Education, 2010) calls for the integration of 21st-century literacies in all aspects of our youth's lives. Yet, from our experiences, technology access is not the only barrier limiting students' use of digital literacies. In some of the communities in which we work, technology is seen as an outside force, a threat to a way of life. For this perspective change to take place, a mental paradigm shift has to occur. The changing demands of the 21st-century literacies requires learners to think and act more flexibly and to assume more responsibility for what and how they learn (Selfe, 2009).

We turned to the literature to investigate how rural youth living in the United States were engaging in 21st-century literacy practices. When we discovered the lack of programs, research, and policy in spite of the government's push for broadband access, we continued to ask questions. Though we do not seek to emphasize the in-school/out-of-school literacies division with this chapter, we seek to add to the growing global conversation around digital literacies (O'Brien & Scharber, 2008). Rural youth's gendered use of technology for multimodal composition as global citizens is a way to address the digital divide "as a reflection of broader social issues" (p. 67).

What Is Rural?

Rural is a contested term: rural sociologists Jacobs & Luloff (1995) explored whether the rural/urban dichotomy was even useful. Data provided by the United States government indicate that approximately 14.7 million of the 72.7 million children living in the United States, live in rural settings (United States Department of Health and Human Services, 2005). However, within the scope of our review, the definition of rural has several connotations. It is important to note the U.S. government's definitions of rural, particularly as defined by institutions such as the U.S. Census Bureau and the Office of Management and Budget. The U.S. Census Bureau classifies anything that is neither an Urbanized Area (50,000 or more people) nor an Urban Cluster (2,500–50,000 people) as rural. The Office of Management and Budget defines anything that is not metropolitan (50,000 or more people) as rural. For those seeking rural grant funding, the definitions of the federal government are essential. However, a monolithic definition of rural is not only limiting to the people who live in rural environments, it hinders visualization of those individuals and their opportunities.

Educational researchers who use qualitative methods often operate from a sociocultural definition of rural. This definition is based on Wirth's (1938) foundational sociological distinction between rural and urban attributions of size of population, density, and heterogeneity, with rural areas being smaller, less densely populated, and more homogeneous. Dewey's (1960) expanded definition included anonymity, division of labor, informal and prescribed relationships, and symbols of status that are independent of personal acquaintance, with rural areas having less of all the indicators.

Whitaker (1983) asserted that the sociocultural definition seemed an "inadequate basis for a satisfactory definition of rural" (p. 73) in education research because of obvious anomalies and suburban communities being defined as rural communities. As was true previously and perhaps increasingly in this century, there are communities of linguistic, ethnic, and occupational diversity in rural areas (Lapping, 1997). Fadiman (1997) told the story of Lia Lee, the Hmong child from a rural California community whose parents struggled with Western medicine's diagnosis and treatment of their daughter's epilepsy. Fink and Dunn (2003) chronicled workers from Guatemala whose presence in a small North Carolina town as workers in a poultry processing plant caused a 900% increase in the need for ESL public services. In the communities in which we work, migrant labor families, predominantly from Central America, share a presence economically, culturally, and linguistically. A sociocultural definition of rural as sparsely populated, relatively homogeneous, occupationally similar, and relationally dependent falls in line with what we experienced as researchers. As a basis from which to launch this chapter, therefore, we combine government population-based and sociocultural definitions of rural.

Access to Technology

Broadband access has become necessary to fully utilize the Internet's potential and to compose and create as an online global citizen; as technologies advance and become more complex, higher data transmission is essential. Without broadband access, those living in rural U.S. settings are left at a disadvantage (Stenberg et al., 2009). The Telecommunications Act of 1996 strove to increase access to broadband communications to rural communities. Within the United States, government-sponsored pilot projects were primarily responsible for building bridges across the digital divide. Organizations such as the Rural Utilities Service, the U.S. Department of Education, and the National Telecommunications and Information Administration funded and administered telecommunications networks in libraries and for various social services, creating hubs for rural communities (Hudson, 2006). In addition, efforts have been made to provide home access to people in rural communities. By 2007, 65% of rural households in the United States with family incomes of $35,000 to $49,000 reported having home computer access to the Internet (National Telecommunications and Information Administration, 2008). However, it appears that people living in rural settings lag behind their peers in urban settings in relation to home computer access to high-speed Internet, with only 70% of people living in rural communities reporting broadband use, while 84% of urban counterparts report having access. While the federal government has sponsored efforts to improve broadband access, it remains difficult for many living in rural communities to obtain. While Internet access has certainly improved in rural communities, youth living in these settings, particularly those from low-income families, still may not have the tools necessary to truly participate in a global community.

Gender and Cosmopolitanism in Rural U.S. Communities

The United Nations Millennium Development Goals (United Nations, 2012) included the promotion of gender equality and the empowerment of women. In target goal 3A, the focus for 2015 is the elimination of disparity in primary and secondary education. Though these goals are set for developing countries, their impact can be felt on developed countries as well. The current poverty statistics in the U.S. reveal "2.8 million children were surviving on $2 or less in income per person per day in a given month" (National Poverty Center, 2012). Comparatively, children in U.S. rural communities suffer from poverty on a larger scale. In 2010 the child poverty rate was 24.4% in nonmetro areas compared to 21.6% in metro areas, and three million more children were in poverty in nonmetro areas in 2010 than in 2008, with signs of increase for the coming year (USDA, 2011). Poverty is a global issue, for the United Nations, and for those working with youth in the U.S., particularly with people in rural communities in the Deep South, Appalachia, and across the Midwest, especially around Native American reservations (Lapping, 1997). Because poverty and the status of women and girls are global policy and research agendas, and because rural U.S. communities resemble the global plight for women and girls, we framed our research questions as follows: How do rural youth negotiate a concept of cosmopolitanism through their online literacy practices? How do rural youth use multimodal composition to construct gender?

As we approached the literature, we found little extant research exploring issues related to rural youth's use of technology to connect to global communities. Literature explores statistics on technology availability and use in rural schools (e.g., Leithner, 2010; Lester, 2012; Shamah & McTavish, 2009), but few studies provide examples of what young people in small communities located in the United States are doing with technologies outside of school contexts. Rural youth deserve our attention for many reasons. First, rural issues simply are not on the map (Howley, 1997); yet, over 20% of American youth live in rural settings (U.S. Department of Health and Human Services, 2005). At the same time, rural youth are often seen as at-risk for leaving rural communities in order to live in more urban areas for economic, social, or cultural reasons, a phenomena known as the "brain drain" (McGranahan, 1991). To challenge this rural flight, a recent report suggests that rural youth who remain in their communities need a more heightened awareness of the community (both local and global) in which they live (Carr & Kefalas, 2009).

The federal government has pushed to provide broadband access to rural communities. With such efforts, one would expect to find information about how rural youth have adopted and adapted technology to connect with the larger world. Without such valuable information, we cannot truly understand how technological advances have influenced and/or change their view of the world and their role in it.

Rural Youths' Participation in Global Communities

Countless versions of Aesop's fable of the country mouse and city mouse exist. The main thrust of these stories is that the character from the city always seems to have what is better and more of it. His country cousin, though impressed, prefers his life because he is safe from the dangers of the city. The media often conflate country or rural with a bucolic life. The stereotypes of those living in rural U.S. as farmers or as people who can grow their own food are also untrue and misleading (Lapping, 1997). Lapping points out that only 2% of the U.S. population are farmers, and that most people in rural communities drive over 10 miles to a grocery store. Lapping refers to much of rural America as "flyover country," in which the people who live are thought to be 'conservative, religiously and socially fundamentalist, and backward" (p. 12). In their look at rural areas as vital and sustainable communities in flux, Donehower et al. (2007) explored "rural literacies" as a framework for doing away with rural stereotypes and for fostering "the particular kinds of literate skills needed to achieve the goals of sustaining life in rural areas" (p. 4). Donehower et al. wanted literacy educators in particular "to examine rural literacies in context and work against the urban biases that inform much of the literacy research in our field" (p. 155). More policy, programs, and research in rural areas to offer as counter evidence for those insisting on the "rhetoric of lack" mythology (p. 27) will help substantiate rural communities as intergenerationally sustainable communities.

From the U.S. Census, it is realistic to create a portrait of a rural youth in the U.S. who is White, Christian, heterosexual, and English-speaking. Those who do not fit this portrait and who live in a rural area may either be in the demographic minority or live in an isolated or small community. The intermingling of cultures and languages in rural areas is increasingly more common, but it is still not the cultural and linguistic norm. The ability to connect through the communication technologies has expanded the world beyond the local community.

In an exploratory study of rural youth and technology, Bauman (2011) surveyed students from one intermediate school that encompasses grades 5–8. According to Bauman, the Arizona community in which the school was located was sparsely populated and the median income was 78% less than the state average, and 23% of the residents lived in poverty. This survey provides valuable insight about the prevalence and use of technology by youth in a rural community. Bauman surveyed 221 students (118 female and 101 male, 2 did not report gender). While the survey did not gather race/ethnicity information, the school website disclosed that 54% of students were Latino, 38% were White, 6% were Native American, and 3% were African American. Of the youth who participated in this study, 60% reported having use of a home computer with Internet access; 78% reported the computer was kept in a public location within the home; 22% reported the computer was kept in the respondent's bedroom, and 48% reported having a personal cellphone. Bauman used a Likert scale to measure students' use of technological activities with 1 representing never and 4 representing very often. Frequency data provided a glimpse of these students' use of technology. Like many of their peers across the country, students reported using email, text messaging, cellphone use, online gaming, shopping, researching information, visiting social media sites, designing websites, blogging and responding to blogs. Frequency of use ranged from 2.43 to 1.25. These youth reported participating in online gaming the most and managing a personal blog the least. No significant differences were found between gender and technology activities (however slightly higher use for girls in email and blogging were noted.) It should be noted that students reported engaging in online activities with peers from their community.

In a second study, Dunn (2011) investigated whether the Internet was making children "less rural." The author used an international study (Laegran, 2002) to frame his work. Using the results of Laegran's study, Dunn (2011) hypothesized that rural children with home Internet access would be more likely to look online for things with which they are already familiar, and the more time rural children use the Internet, the more likely they will be to chat with people online. The author surveyed third-graders from a school in a rural Northern Florida County. The survey primarily consisted of a 25-item survey which mainly incorporated a 4-point Likert scale. Of the children surveyed, 80.2% had home Internet access. Time spent online (M=2.83) was measured using a Likert scale, 1 (never) to 4 (every day).

Dunn's findings supported his hypothesis. Children who had the Internet at home were more likely to search about things they liked and/or had heard about than things with which they were unfamiliar. In addition, the participants who used the Internet more frequently were more likely to chat online; however, the reported data was insufficient to determine with whom the participants interacted with online. In other words, the survey data did not clarify whether the participants were chatting with friends from their hometown or people with whom they did not have a previous relationship,

Both studies cited are of a small scale; however, they do provide some insight concerning rural youth's use of technology to partake in a global society. The data from Bauman's study (2011) suggest that rural youth use technology to engage in online activities to meet with others in virtual spaces. Youth in these studies used information communication technologies to learn about the world in which they live and interact with others. Dunn's study (2011) builds on the work of Bauman. Like Bauman, Dunn used survey research to measure rural youth's use of ICTs. The data from Dunn's study reaffirms that rural youth use the Internet to participate in online activities that connect them to the larger world.

Rural Youth's Multimodal Composition and Gender Construction

Cosmopolitanism, as a concept, was initially used by the Stoics to describe a "citizen of the world." Unterhalter (2008) wrote that cosmopolitanism encourages "different ways to understand global interconnections and some of the intellectual resources provided by cosmopolitanism for understanding gender equality in education as a global issue" (p. 551). The idea of working toward equal rights for all can be disconcerting for some, however: "The privileging of gender relations and patriarchy above other social forms of power (e.g. those of age, rural–urban, caste, ethnicity or race) do not translate easily across societies" (Arnot & Fennell, 2008, p. 6). However, as Arnot and Fennell pointed out, gender parity goals such as those promoted by the MDGs are the catalyst that provide rural communities worldwide access to Internet technologies and connect young people as equal contributors to a global community. Efforts to assert gender equality are often more public in developing countries, and research on rural young women's online literacy practices is on the increase. Because the U.S. is considered developed and because, often, rural girls and women are overlooked as in need of active campaigns and efforts for targeted education campaigns, the programs and resultant research go unfunded. Nevertheless, there are quality programs in progress. One example in the Appalachian mountains of North Carolina is a joint effort with Duke University and the Madison County School System: Professor Deborah Hicks runs the Spring Creek Literacy Project, a K–12 literacy initiative that culminates in a six-week summer program for middle-grades girls. Hicks (Spring Creek Literacy Project, 2010) describes these rural youths as "girls between time" engaged in capturing their lives through the old tradition of mountain storytelling and new literacies of digital storytelling (p. 6). With the assistance of students from Duke University, the girls write short stories, personal narratives, and poems, and compile their writing and personal photographs in an ebook, which is online for public viewing.

Construction of gender in online spaces already has a research tradition (Guzzetti & Gamboa, 2005; Hull & Schultz, 2002). For those youth living in rural areas who are not of the dominant sexual orientation, the idea of multimodal composition through online sources provided outlets not previously known. In a study of LGBTQ youth living in rural Appalachia, Gray (2009) found that the Internet provided young people access to "genres of queer realness" that their urban counterparts were exposed to on a daily basis (p. 1172). Sites such as PlanetOut and Gay.com served as connecting points for young people seeking coming-out stories. Online commercial outlets for buying LGBTQ accessories provided the tools young people used to publicly claim identity. Other young people's homepages, regional discussion boards, and news bulletins from organizations such as the National Gay and Lesbian Task Force were also cited by the young people as influential in their identity formation.

Often, young LGBTQ people growing up in rural areas are doubly stigmatized because "the way rurality itself is depicted is antithetical to LGBTQ identities" (Gray, 2009, p. 1165). A "politics of visibility" that is common among urban youth is often shunned in rural communities where heteronormative family values are prized. And though Internet cafes, schools, and government offices have increased access for those who lack the Internet at home, filters keep LGBTQ youth from exploring those sites that help make their queerness real. Even for those who had access at home, Gray noted that the economic issues with working poor and lower-middle-class youth led to shared computers and privacy issues, so they could not search without fear of being caught.

Family was extremely important to the young people in Gray's (2009) study, and their "stories resonate with the complex negotiation of visibility and main-taining family ties that consume rural young people's everyday lives" (p. 1172). Family, in rural tradition, is said to have a rigid structure, with the stereotype holding the conservative two-parent household, male breadwinner as the model. However, recent studies of rural family structures have found more gender flexibility than previously thought. For example, Sherman (2009) found that factory closings can damage "male identity and self-esteem, and also can destabilize the existing gender order of communities" (p. 601). However, she found that men were able to be flexible in their gender roles, adjusting and readjusting their expectations for being the head-of-the-household and sole provider when the sawmill closed due to environmental restrictions because of the spotted owl in Northern California. Because none of the young people in Gray's study wanted to leave their rural settings, they made their identities fit the framework of their family. Using the information they found on the Internet, they recontextualized their concept of family and their roles in them.

Implications For Future Research and Instruction

We found very little extant literature on the multimodal literacy practices of rural youth. Swayed by our work with rural schools and rural youth, we find this lack of research disconcerting. With nearly 15 million children living in rural com-munities, we feel it is time for rural youth's use of technology and engagement in a global community to be on the map.

Survey research can build on the existing work of Baumann (2011) and Dunn (2011). Additional small-scale surveys can provide snapshots of youth's practices in specific rural communities; however, a large-scale national survey of rural youth's multimodal composition practices would be valuable for researchers, educators, and policymakers alike.

The research we have found indicates that the introduction of new literacies and the opportunity for multimodal composition practices have aided both opportunities for and increased public perception of rural youth's flexible gender roles. Additional qualitative studies could provide further insight about how rural youth utilize multimodal compositions to construct their gender identity.

References

Arnot, M. (2009). A global conscience collective? Incorporating gender injustice into global citizenship education. *Education, Citizenship and Social Justice, 4,* 117–132.

Arnot, M. & Fennell, S. (2008). Gendered education and national development: critical perspectives and new research. *Compare: Journal of Comparative Education, 38,* 515–523.

Baumann, S. (2011). Cyberbullying in a rural intermediate school: An exploratory study. *The Journal of Early Adolescence, 30,* 803–833.

Carr, P.J. & Kefalas, M.J. (2009, September 21). The rural brain drain. The Chronicle of Higher Education. Retrieved from www.chronicle.com/artiicle/the-Rural-Brain-Drain/48425/

Daniell, B. & Mortensen, P. (2007). *Women and literacy: Local and global inquiries for a new century.* New York: Lawrence Erlbaum Associates.

Dewey, R. (1960) The rural-urban continuum: Real but relatively unimportant. *American Journal of Sociology, 66,* 60–66.

Donehower, K., Hogg, C., & Schell, E.E. (2007). *Rural literacies.* Carbondale: Southern Illinois University Press.

Dunn, R.A. (2011). Is the Web making children less rural? A study of the Internet's impact on non-urban youth. *Journal of Rural Community Psychology.* Retrieved from http://www.marshall.edu/jrcp/PDFVOL/14.2%20-%20Dunn.pdf

Fadiman, A. (1997). The spirit catches you and you fall down: A Hmong child, her American doctors, and the collision of two cultures. New York: Farrar, Straus, & Giroux.

Fink, L. & Dunn, A.E. (2003). The Maya of Morganton: Work and community in the nuevo new south. Chapel Hill, NC: University of North Carolina Press.

Graham, S. & Marvin, S. (1996). *Telecommunications and the city: Electronic spaces, urban places.* London: Routledge.

Gray, M.L. (2009). Negotiating identities/queering desires: Coming out online and the remediation of the coming-out story. *Journal Of Computer-Mediated Communication,14*(4), 1162–1189. doi:10.1111/j.1083-6101.2009.01485.x

Guzzetti, B. & Gamboa, M. (2005). Online journaling: The informal writings of two adolescent girls. *Research in the Teaching of English 40*: 168–206.

Howley, C.B. (1997). Studying the rural in education: Nation-building, "globalization," and school improvement.

Hudson, H.E. (2006). From rural village to global village: Telecommunications for development in the information age. Mahwah, NJ: Lawrence Erlbaum Associates.

Hull, G. & K. Schultz (2002). *School's out: Bridging out-of-school literacies with classroom practices.* New York: Teachers College Press.

Jacobs, S. & Luloff, A.E. (1995). Exploring the meaning of rural through cognitive maps. *Rural Sociology 60,* 260–273.

Laegran, A.S. (2002). The petrol state and the Internet café: Rural technospaces or youth. *Journal of Rural Studies, 18,* 157–168,

Lapping, M.B. (1997). A tradition of rural sustainability: The Amish portrayed. In I. Audirac (Ed.) *Rural sustainable development in America* (pp. 29–40). New York: John Wiley.

Leithner, A. (2010). Internet enriches cultural education in rural areas. Retrieved from news.change.org/stories/internet-enriches-cultural-education-inrural-areas

Lester, L. (2012). Putting rural readers on the map: Strategies for rural literacy. *The Reading Teacher, 65,* 401–441.

McGranahan, D.A. (1991). Education and rural economic development: Strategies for the 1990s. Washington, DC: U.S. Department of Agriculture.

National Poverty Center (2012). Poverty in the United States: Frequently asked questions. Retrieved http://npc.umich.edu/

National Telecommunications and Information Administration. (2008). Networked nation: Broadband in America 2007. Retrieved from http://www.ntia.doc.gov/report/2008/networked-nation-broadband-america-2007

Nussbaum, M. (2002) Education for citizenship in an era of global connection. *Studies in Philosophy and Education, 21*, 289–303.

O'Brien, D. & Scharber, C. (2008). Digital literacies go to school: Potholes and possibilities. *Journal of Adolescent and Adult Literacy 52*, 66–68.

Selfe, C.L. (2009). The movement of air, the breath of meaning: Aurality and multimodal composing. *College Compositon and Communication 60*, 616–663.

Shamah, D. & McTavish, K.A. (2009). Rural research brief: Making room for place based knowledge in rural classrooms. *Rural Educator, 30*(2), 1–4.

Sherman, J. (2009). Bend to avoid breaking: Job loss, gender norms, and family stability in rural America. *Social Problems, 56*(4), 599–620.

Spring Creek Literacy Project. (2010). Girls between time. Retrieved from http://www.springcreekliteracyproject.com/magazine.html

Stenberg, P., Morehart,M., Vogel, S., Cromartie, J.,Breneman,V., & Brown, D. (2009). Broadband Internet's value for rural America. U.S. Department of Agriculture: Washington, DC.

Stone, A.R. (1992). Will the real body please stand up? Boundary stories about virtual cultures. In: Benedikt, M. (Eds.), Cyberspace: First steps. Cambridge, MA: MIT Press.

United Nations (2012). Millennium goals. Retrieved from http://www.un.org/millennium goals/

United States Census Bureau (2010). Urban and rural classification and urban area criteria. Retrieved from http://www.census.gov/geo/www/ua/2010urbanruralclass.html

United States Department of Agriculture. (2011). Rural income, poverty, and welfare: Poverty demographics. Retrieved from http://www.ers.usda.gov/Briefing/Income PovertyWelfare/PovertyDemographics.htm

United States Department of Education. (2010). National education technology plan. Retrieved http://www.ed.gov/technology/netp-201

United States Department of Health and Human Services (2005). Retrieved from http://www.hhs.gov/

Unterhalter, E. (2008). Cosmopolitanism, global social justice and gender equality in education. *Compare: A Journal Of Comparative Education, 38*(5), 539–553.

Valentine, G. & Holloway, S.L. (2001). A window to a wider world? Rural children's use of information and communication technologies. *Journal of Rural Studies, 17*, 383–394.

Whitaker, W. (1983). Conceptualizing "rural" for research in education: A sociological perspective. *Rural Education, 1* (1): 71–76.

Wirth, L. (1938). Urbanism as a way of life. *American Journal of Sociology, 44*; 3–24.

11

A NEW LOOK AT GIRLS, GAMING, AND LITERACIES

Elisabeth R. Hayes

Until recently, the suggestion that girls, video gaming, and literacy might have something to do with each other would have been considered somewhat outlandish. Video gaming has long been associated with teenage boys, and typically assumed to have a deleterious effect on literacy and literacy development (Steinkuehler, 2007). Today, however, girls are playing games in increasing numbers due to games that are more appealing to females. There is also increasing recognition that video gaming incorporates a wide range of literacy practices, from reading and writing traditional texts to meaning making that scholars have described as gaming literacy (Gee, 2007; Steinkuehler, 2007; Zimmerman, 2008).

Girls vary in their gaming practices, and the literacies involved in these practices vary considerably as well. Girls have different patterns of gaming than boys although there is overlap in the games girls and boys play and the literacies they potentially acquire. The most significant gender-related differences are the tendencies of boys and men to play games more frequently, for longer periods of time, to play different sorts of games than girls and women, and to own their own consoles. Boys tend to be more engaged in the social practices and communities associated with gaming than girls (Lenhart et al., 2008). One reason for these differences may be the ongoing association of shooting, fighting, and military-themed gaming with masculinity; such games still have hyper-sexualized representations of women and male players are at times still openly hostile to women. There is also an ongoing predominance of men in computer science reflected in the smaller numbers of girls and women who participate in the more highly technical practices associated with gaming, such as modding (Hayes, 2008). Notably, games designed specifically for girls tend to be aimed at younger children, are less complex, and focus on stereotypical content, such as fashion or makeovers.

In the next section, I develop a view of gaming as a collection of social practices that include but go beyond game play (Gee & Hayes, 2009, 2010). This perspective demonstrates how literacy is implicated in terms of how players use various forms of texts to support gaming practices, what I will call "print literacies," as well as how gaming involves consuming and producing meanings in a broader sense, what I call "gaming literacies." I then discuss several different examples of practices associated with the popular computer game *The Sims* to illustrate these literacies. As I conclude, literacy educators have a role to play in enhancing both forms of literacy, although this will require them to be more cognizant of how gender has affected their own views of the literacies involved in gaming.

A Social Practice View of Gaming

As Lankshear and Knobel (2003) and other scholars associated with the New Literacy Studies argue, literacy is always embedded in social practices that give value to particular ways of producing and consuming texts (New London Group, 1996). A New Literacy Studies approach also broadens our conception of "texts" to include multimodal, increasingly digital forms of representation that can be as varied as a game interface or machinima (movies set within and acted out within video games). Literacy as part of social practices is integrated with different ways of acting and interacting, different ways of knowing, valuing, and believing and, often, different ways of using various sorts of tools and technologies.

To understand the social practices of gaming it is necessary to consider the broad scope of video games. Modern-day video gaming involves a considerable diversity of game genres, played on platforms ranging from handheld devices such as cellphones to computers to game consoles such as the Wii, Xbox 360 and the Playstation 3. Game genres are defined by particular patterns of game play, and range from first-person shooters and role-playing games to puzzle games and sports games. The addition of motion sensor devices to game consoles has expanded the physical aspects of gaming to include dance, exercise, and performance games. Content also varies in age-appropriateness and theme, from games that simulate warfare or other violent actions to those that involve caring for a virtual pet or managing a restaurant. The stereotype of a "gamer" as a socially awkward teenage boy playing first-person shooters alone in his basement is clearly a thing of the past.

Understanding gaming, or how literacy is involved in gaming, requires more than just analyzing various game genres or content. Games are played differently by individual players as well as by multiple players in a multiplayer game. How games are played is tied in part to the physical and social context of gaming. Many games are designed to be played with other people, either online or in the same room. In addition to game play itself, people participate in a wide range of *social interactions* around gaming—they discuss games, online and offline, share game play strategies and achievements. Some players also engage in *production* around gaming, such as creating new content for games, producing video walkthroughs of game play, and other artifacts. Another aspect of gaming as a social practice are the *identities* associated with gaming, including the identities we associate with being a "gamer." Some players identify with a particular kind of game that they like to play, i.e. "I'm a Starcraft fan," while others are identified with a level of skills or commitment: "She's a newb" (newcomer) or "He's a really hardcore gamer."

The identities and practices associated with gaming continue to be gendered; boys and men are more likely to use gaming as a means of bonding with friends, parents are more likely to buy game consoles for boys, and more game genres appeal to boys than girls. Girls on the whole do tend to be more casual gamers than boys, but that may be a consequence of the lack of appealing games, little parental support, and stereotypes about gaming. The more sophisticated and complex gaming practices that girls and women do participate in may be rendered invisible by their association with topics and concerns that most game designers— and researchers—may dismiss as trivial. *The Sims*, for example, a popular game among girls and women, has been described in a rather dismissive way as "the new dollhouse" because it focuses on managing the needs of digital people and families (Schiesel, 2006).

Literacies and Gaming

An expansive, social practice view of gaming provides a broad way to think about literacies in relationship to gaming. For the purpose of this discussion, I draw on two different conceptualizations of literacy: print literacies and gaming literacies. *Print literacies* in relation to gaming refers to making meaning of the various forms of written language that are part and parcel of gaming. Written texts can be found within a game, like popup menus that explain in-game actions or provide information about characters and plot. There also are texts beyond the game itself that support game play and social interaction, such as manuals, player-created walkthroughs, online game discussion forums, and even fan fiction (Steinkuehler, 2007). Often these texts are multimodal; meaning is constructed through a variety of modalities (images, symbols, sound, spatiality, etc.), not just words.

The concept of *gaming literacy* represents another way to understand literacy in relation to gaming. From this more expansive perspective, games are complex sociotechnical systems; literacy involves "reading the game," or understanding how the game works to play successfully. Gaming literacy also involves the ability to critique games in terms of their playability or innovation; understanding the conventions of different game genres; and being aware of and able to critique the cultural models underlying game content and design (Gee, 2007; Gee & Hayes, 2009).

Gaming literacy involves a form of production ("writing") in terms of the player's ability to modify existing games and game play and create new games (Zimmerman, 2008). Some games have built-in tools that allow players to modify games and game play; players may hack into the underlying game code to redesign the game interface and even create entirely new games. Gaming literacy as reflected in these practices includes requisite technical production skills, an understanding of games as systems comprised of computer-generated rules, and the ability to design a human play experience for a particular cultural and social context. Gaming literacy represents a potentially crucial set of 21st-century skills and knowledge (Zimmerman, 2008).

The Literacies of Game Play

Playing any video game typically requires the player to make meaning of a complex combination of print, icons, and toolbars that comprise the game interface. Often information is presented in layers; icons on the main level can be clicked to bring up more detailed texts related to gameplay. In *The Sims 3*, for example, the main user interface consists primarily of icons that let the player perform basic functions, like changing views and using camera or video tools, and monitoring the current sim's moods (a "sim" is a virtual person in the game). Clicking on an arrow brings up a set of detailed panels with more information about the sim's personality, needs, and other attributes.

Interpreting these "texts" requires mastery of what Gee (2007) calls the "semiotic domain" of the game; that is, the ways that different modalities are organized and used to communicate distinctive meanings, in this case associated with the particular mechanics and goals of *The Sims* and with video games more broadly. There are some general conventions associated with games, such as the use of icons and slider bars to convey meaning in a condensed format, and other design features specific to an individual game. As an example, *Sims* game play includes three separate modes, Building, Buying, and Live mode (when the real action of the game takes place); each mode has its own interface with different icons, texts, and functions.

What is significant about these game play literacies? First, texts in games are quite different from the kinds of texts that are typically found in school. A game interface is designed for action, "reading to do" rather than "reading to learn" with no immediate application. Written language is de-emphasized, although it is still present, and in more copious quantities than might be immediately apparent. Literacy texts commonly valued in school are woven throughout the game, such as classification schemes, complex vocabulary, and texts combined with numeric information. For instance, *The Sims 3* has a Skill Journal with information, statistics, and challenges associated with each skill (such as Charisma, Athletic, Gardening, Handiness, and more) that a sim is developing. The Skill Journal for Handiness, for example (the ability to fix things in the game, like broken toilets), displays statistics on seven actions related to the skill, such as number of objects repaired and percent of unique upgrades completed, and descriptions of challenges that lead to enhanced skills. These descriptions include criteria and definitions, like this one for Tinkerer (one of the skill levels that is part of Handiness):

Tinkerers have finished at least 10 unique upgrades on household items. Installing the "Unbreakable" upgrade on multiple objects only counts as one unique upgrade, so it helps to experiment with different upgrade options!

(The Sims 3, 2009)

Playing *The Sims* successfully requires a particular kind of gaming literacy that is easy to underestimate if the game is viewed simply as a "dollhouse." From the start, *The Sims* engages players as designers or co-creators of their game play (Gee, 2007). Players are offered a myriad of choices, including selecting or creating neighborhoods, houses, families and individual sims. One of the first tasks a player confronts is how to understand and limit the game's complexity to avoid catastrophes such as burning down a house, having the children taken away by social services, or furnishing a home without essential features like toilets or fire detectors. To manage this complexity, the player must begin to develop an awareness of how the game functions as a system, understand (implicitly or explicitly) that the game is governed by a set of underlying rules, and how those rules operate in the game.

The Literacies of Creating Game Content

A popular practice associated with *The Sims* (and many other games) is creating new content for the game. *The Sims* offers players the ability to customize their sims and design new clothes and buildings with in-game tools. Players can also create new content with other software tools like Photoshop (http://www. photoshop.com/) and Gimp (http://www.gimp.org/), and then import the content into their games. The literacies involved with such practices are associated with the tools themselves which often have quite complex interfaces, and the documentation around the tools, such as tutorials, software manuals, and forum discussions. The particular form of literacy associated with these practices is the acquisition and use of specialist forms of language (Hayes & Lee, 2012). Specialist language involves not only distinctive terminology, but also characteristic ways of making knowledge claims, establishing social relationships, and expressing identities. In school, the acquisition of specialist language is central to learning disciplinary content; in *Sims* content creation, specialist language is often associated with computing tools that girls in particular might not be exposed to otherwise.

Game literacy is tied closely to being able to move across different software programs to move and manipulate content, and the ability to discuss these processes with other players/content creators. One aspect of game literacy is not just creating content for the game, but creating tutorials—written or video—that address common practices in a form interpretable to other players. This requires not only a knowledge of the game, but of the game community, the perspective of players new to the practice, and common problems they might encounter; i.e., the interaction between player and software.

The Literacies of Game Fan Fiction

Fan fiction is a literacy practice associated with many forms of popular media, including video games (see www.fanfiction.com for examples of many types of fan fiction). Fan fiction, simply put, is stories about characters or settings written by fans of the original work, rather than by the original creator. While much fan fiction is purely print-based, *The Sims* has spawned a distinctive form of multimodal storytelling in which players combine screen shots and text to create narratives that can be uploaded and shared with other fans on the *Sims* game site (Lammers et al., 2009). *Sims* fan fiction can take many forms, ranging from vampire romances to historical dramas. Typically, players combine a small amount of text with a screen shot to create a "page" of story, and publish stories in the form of chapters that each may include dozens of pages. *The Sims 3* has a Create a Story tool on the game website that lets players upload images, add text, customize background and audio, and share with other players. Sometimes players will post *Sims* fan fiction in the form of blogs; one of the more widely read stories created with *The Sims 3* was Alice and Kev, (http://aliceandkev.wordpress.com/), a story about a homeless father and daughter created by a female student of game design in the UK. Players have created entire fan sites devoted to *Sims* fan fiction, complete with writing tips, editorial assistance, and contests. The skills involved in creating *Sims* fan fiction include not just story writing, but also using various techniques to attract and keep an audience, such as creating engaging titles, designing forum "signatures" that advertise a story, responding to fan comments, and serving as an editor for other authors.

The game literacies involved in creating these multimodal stories are substantial. To illustrate their stories, players must create appropriate sims and design suitable in-game settings. Some players create custom sims and other content to make their characters distinctive or to represent a particular setting. Beyond creating custom content, players also must learn to position sims for good screen shots. Screenshots may be imported into Photoshop or other software. Not only does the player need to understand the game well enough to anticipate what scenes can be created, he or she also must develop a sort of "design literacy" to combine images and text to be mutually reinforcing and compelling to the intended audience.

The Literacies of Game Challenges

Creating and completing "challenges" is a distinctive practice associated with *The Sims* that incorporates both print and game literacies. Challenges have specific goals and conditions, and typically are created by players to provide a new game play experience that tests players' skills. This is a popular form of game play in *The Sims* community; players have created fan sites and discussion groups devoted entirely to *Sims* challenges. Challenges bear some similarities to other forms of game modification in which players create new versions of a game through modifying or modding the game software. In the case of *Sims* challenges, players do not modify the game software but create rules that players must follow while completing the goal. One popular, long-lasting *Sims* challenge is "The Legacy Challenge," that requires a player to play a family through ten generations.

Print literacies associated with challenges include writing and interpreting the challenge goals and rules, and discussing the challenge with other players. Players often report on their progress toward completing a challenge in the form of a story by using images and text similar to the *Sims* fan fiction described in the previous section. Creating a *Sims* challenge involves game literacy: knowing enough about how the game works to identify a situation or storyline that might be simulated in the game, and setting parameters on game play so it provides an enjoyable, meaningful, and stimulating experience for others.

Implications for Literacy Education

The examples in this chapter are intended to suggest the richness of literacies tied to various practices associated with a popular game among girls and women. If nothing else, educators can take away a new appreciation for how gaming might serve as a hub for a wide variety of new and traditional forms of literacy for girls as well as boys. Young people of both sexes may be potentially engaged in sophisticated literacy practices associated with gaming that are currently invisible to educators and policymakers alike. Scholars such as Lankshear and Knobel (2003) have called for fostering stronger connections across multiple sites of literacy learning; these sites should include games and game-related spaces. Teachers, many of whom are female and who don't identify as gamers, may need professional development opportunities that expose them to the literacy learning potential of gaming. In a recent survey of preservice teachers, I and my co-author (Hayes & Ohrnberger, 2012) found that less than half of respondents currently played video games; even more importantly, they reported very little engagement with online game communities and only occasional use of game-related resources, suggesting that they might have limited exposure to the wide range of literacy practices associated with gaming.

A second implication is that girls' (and boys') engagement in these game-related literacy practices varies considerably, and only a small proportion are engaged in the most sophisticated forms of game content creation (Hayes, 2008). In my own work with girls and games, I found that many did not have access to the tools, adult mentoring and peer support that are important in fostering the sophisticated literacy skills associated with gaming. Educators and parents can leverage the potential of games for literacy development among girls as well as boys. For example, in one program we introduced middle-school-age girls to *Sims* fan fiction sites, read and discussed *Sims* stories together, and taught the girls the basics of Photoshop so they could design covers for their own *Sims* stories. They also created blogs to document their game play and learned to upload screenshots to illustrate their posts. The advantage of *Sims* fan fiction and blogs, as opposed to simply print-based writing, was that the girls were able to develop skills with new media and design in combination with textual forms of expression.

Finally, an appreciation of the literacies associated with gaming may help teachers and researchers broaden their conceptions of valuable literacies in school. In particular, the notion of gaming literacies suggests a way of thinking about games as dynamic, designed, systems of meaning with valuable 21st-century literacies that students may not be developing in or out of school. These literacies may be crucial to increasing the participation of girls in STEM fields, where they are still underrepresented, and helping them become more engaged producers with, as well as consumers of, digital media.

References

Gee, J.P. (2007). *What video games have to teach us about learning and literacy.* (2nd ed.). New York: Palgrave/Macmillan.

Gee, J.P. & Hayes, E.R. (2009). "No quitting without saving after bad events": Gaming paradigms and learning in *The Sims. International Journal of Learning & Media, 1*(3), 1–17.

Gee, J. & Hayes, E. (2010). *Women as gamers: The Sims and 21st century learning.* New York: Palgrave Macmillan.

Hayes, E. (2008). Game content creation and IT proficiency: An exploratory study. *Computers and Education, 51*(1), 97–108.

Hayes, E. & Gee, J.P. (2010). No selling the genie lamp: A game literacy practice in *The Sims. E-learning, 7*(1), 67–78.

Hayes, E. & King, E. (2009). Not just a dollhouse: What *The Sims 2* can teach us about women's IT learning. *On the Horizon 17*(1), 60–69.

Hayes, E. & Lee, Y. (2012). Specialist language acquisition and trajectories of IT learning in a Sims fan site. In Hayes, E. & Duncan, S. (Eds.). *Video games, affinity spaces and new media literacies.* New York: Peter Lang.

Hayes, E. & Ohrnberger, M. (2012). *The gamer generation teaches school: The gaming practices of pre-service teachers.* Paper presented at the American Educational Research Association Conference, Vancouver, Canada, April 2012.

Lammers, J., Lee, Y., & Hayes, E. (2009). *Reading the game: Traditional and new literacy practices in The Sims 2.* Paper presented at the American Educational Research Association Conference, San Diego, CA.

Lankshear, C. & Knobel, M. (2003). *New literacies: Changing knowledge and classroom learning.* Buckingham, UK: Open University Press.

Lenhart, A., Kahn, J., Middaugh, E., Macgill, A., Evans, C., & Vitak, J. (2008). *Teens, video games, and civics.* Washington: Pew Internet and American Life Project. Retrieved from: http://www.pewinternet.org/Reports/2008/Teens-Video-Games-and-Civics.aspx

New London Group. (1996). A pedagogy of multiliteracies: Designing social futures. *Harvard Educational Review, 66*(1), 60–92.

Schiesel, S. (2006, May 7). Welcome to the new dollhouse. *The New York Times.* Available at: www.nytimes.com/2006/05/07/arts/07schi.html?_r 1/4 1andoref 1/4 slogin

Steinkuehler, C. (2007). Massively multiplayer online gaming as a constellation of literacy practices, *E-Learning 4*(3), 297–318.

Zimmerman, E. (2008). Gaming literacy: Game design as a model for literacy in the 21st century. In B. Perron. & M.J.P. Wolf (Eds.) *The Video Game Theory Reader 2* (pp. 23–31). New York: Routledge.

PART III
Gender and Literacy: Issues and Policies

12

THE GIRL CITIZEN-READER

Gender and Literacy Education for 21st-Century Citizenship

Judith Dunkerly and Helen Harper

The nature of citizenship in the 21st century is changing. Technological advancement, and changing social and economic circumstances are forging new and multiple alliances and allegiances in a closer, more transient, interdependent and global world (Harper et al., 2011). Some argue that a notion of global rather than national citizenship can better meet the social, economic, technological, and ecological challenges and circumstances of our times (Apple et al., 2005; Banks, 2004; Edwards & Usher, 2000/2008; Kenway & Langmead, 2000). A small but growing number of scholars are promoting rethinking literacy education in light of global citizenship and cosmopolitan sensibilities (Harper et al., 2011; Goldstein, 2007; Tierney, 2006; Luke, 2002, 2004).

Feminist scholars note the gendered nature not only of literacy education, but also of citizenship, global or otherwise (Kenway & Langmead, 2000; Arnot & Dillabough, 2000; Benhabib, 1995). As eminent political scholar, Seyla Benhabib (1995) observed, the notion of a female citizen "is embedded in a set of tensions over securing equality with males and preserving and honoring women's difference" (pp. 29–30). Perhaps the most basic and most vexing tension exists in the public/private split of citizenship. Historically, citizenship has been largely understood, articulated and enacted in the public/political sphere, which has not easily admitted or recognized women who have been confined to or more active in, and/or viewed as more "naturally" affiliated with the private/domestic sphere. The responsibilities and activities of marriage and motherhood have not been easily tied to the identity of the citizen. Dillabough (2000) suggests that in most Western countries female citizenship has been constituted as a "feeble enterprise because 'to be a woman' has typically implied the opposite of citizenship" (p. 163). She comments further, "To engage in the work of the private sphere—motherhood, caring, service has been to invoke the status of the non-citizen or non-worker"

(p. 164). Moreover the activities of the private sphere were thought not to demand the highly rationalized thinking and education required in the public/political sphere of the (male) citizen worker. At best, women were viewed as the medium through which the state and its members would be nurtured. Thus, the role of female teachers, for example, would be ideologically and symbolically, "to cultivate citizenship in the young, to keep intact the political machinery of liberal democracy rather than acquiring citizenship status themselves" (Dillabough, 2000; p. 162). Women become "the keepers of liberal democracy," yet, historically have been precluded from citizenship status (Walkerdine & Lucey, 1989).

Although challenged by various social and political movements through much of the 20th century, basic framing of the citizen and of gender has a legacy in contemporary institutional cultures that divide and differentiate individuals and shape their citizenship identities accordingly. Schools, one such cultural institution, have played an important role in shaping contemporary male–female relations, and in shaping male–female citizenship. Thus, "education has become an important site of conflict over the meaning of citizenship, particularly as it concerns girls and women" (Arnot and Dillabough, 2000, pp. 5–6). Considering the alignment of literacy and citizenship, as well as the gendered nature of school literacy experiences (Johnson, 2000; Smith, 2000; Twomey, 2007) our premise is that school literacy plays an important role in the shaping of female/male identities and by extension female/male citizenship identities. In light of the new and emerging emphasis on global citizenship, the time seems ripe to reconsider how citizenship, gender, and literacy education might be reconfigured in ways to support girls' global citizenship in a changing world. To begin such reconceptualizing work, in this chapter we examine two agencies concerned with global life that focus on girls' literacy education, in a search for ways of rethinking and reinvigorating local literacy education to support the "girl citizen-reader" of the 21st century (Spring, 2004). For the purposes of this research, the term "girl citizen-reader" is utilized to represent and concretize a position/identity we are attempting to promote through this line of inquiry. The "girl citizen-reader" refers to young women who can and will use literacy, in the words of Paulo Freire, to "read the word and the world" in ways that support democratic citizenship lived locally, in either the public and/or private spheres, but most importantly framed within a global context (Beck, 2002, Harper et al., 2011). We deploy the term "girl citizen-reader" rather than Dillabough's (2000) "girl citizen-worker" to highlight the role and importance of literacy practices, required in the development and enactment of citizenship.

The Agencies in Brief

In reconceptualizing the literacy education needed by the 21st-century girl citizen-reader we examine how she is already being configured in two international sites where gender, literacy and citizenship and global circumstances meet: UNESCO and USAID. Both international agencies are concerned with education in general and literacy in particular, and have policies and initiatives focused on girls and young women. Similarly, their histories and original purposes have a global perspective that influences the ways in which they position, name and support (or not) the girl citizen-reader.

UNESCO

The United Nations Educational, Scientific and Cultural Organization (UNESCO) is a specialized agency of the United Nations. With regard to education, the overriding goal of UNESCO is to improve the education of children, youth, and adults worldwide, by working as an intellectual leader, catalyst, resource, broker, and monitor to provide expertise and to foster partnerships to strengthen national educational leadership and the capacity of countries to offer quality education for all populations. At this time, the major priority of UNESCO's education initiatives is "Education for All" (EFA) which involves the provision of free, compulsory primary education for all children by 2015.

USAID

With regard to education, the U.S. Aid for International Development organization (USAID) supports efforts in developing countries to improve education. It also has initiatives addressing teacher education and curriculum development. Specific programs designed to support the education of girls, and other marginalized populations are directly referenced: "As a matter of policy, USAID places major emphasis on female access to basic education. In all cases, USAID emphasizes educational equity for girls and women as a strategy for achieving educational equality for all." USAID's Education Strategy: Improving Lives through Learning, 2009). As an independent federal agency, USAID also participates in UNESCO's Education for All initiative. In keeping with its stated goals of furthering U.S. economic interests, USAID emphasizes the role of education in producing a workforce that is knowledgeable, skilled, and able to contribute to a global economy.

Our Purpose and Methods

We conducted a close reading of international texts to examine the ways in which international education policies shape the global discourse on literacy in general, and its use by girls and women, in particular. Specifically, we were guided by the concept that language—whether written or oral—is never neutral. It is politicized, positioned, and reflects the interests of the speaker/writer/entity (Fairclough, 2000). Our analysis centered on studying and interpreting texts with the purpose of uncovering the discursive sources of power, dominance, inequality, and bias.

Data sources for this research were drawn from public online and print documents centering on literacy education from: (1) UNESCO, concerning literacy programs and policies pertaining to female students; and (2) educational documents produced by USAID that have explicit reference to the literacy education of girls internationally. Although both agencies have produced scores of documents relating to education policy, programs and practice, the documents we reviewed were chosen using the following criteria: the documents had to (1) address literacy education specifically, (2) name or have implications for female students, and (3) address directly or indirectly local, national and/or global citizenship. In examining the documents, we analyzed the positioning of girls with regard to citizenship and literacy education, drawing on Foucauldian notions of discursive power, regimes of truth; and what Foucault calls "governmentality": a reference to how individuals regulate themselves within discursive bounds of what constitutes "normal" (Foucault, 1980, 1991, 2000). We looked for what was rendered normal and legitimate in relation to what was understood as good literacy education and good citizenship for girls within the context of global/cosmopolitan 21st-century life.

Our Findings

There was considerable variation in the discourse concerning citizenship, literacy education, and gender across and within our sources. Taken together, however, they offer some insights and possibilities for rethinking girls' literacy education locally and nationally.

The UNESCO Documents

Of some surprise, the UNESCO documents did not name or address the nature of the global/cosmopolitan citizenship directly. However, universal human rights, often a supporting sidebar to global citizenship, were emphasized. The UNESCO/UNICEF documents on the Education for All initiative, and, most notably, UNICEF's "A Human Rights-Based Approach to Education for All" (2007) were framed entirely on naming education and the literacy it brings as a universal human right. A global citizen (while not referenced directly), referred to all people everywhere, all of whom are in possession of universal human rights and as such cannot be denied access to schooling and literacy education, which is explicitly named as one of these rights.

Girls and young women are named as those most likely to have their right to education and literacy violated, through sexual and gender harassment, and in penalties, including expulsion for becoming pregnant as a result of an early marriage (Tomasevski, 2003). The girl citizen-reader, is positioned as an individual whose rights are being denied and therefore whose citizenship is threatened. Equality with males is critical in the UNESCO documents (Samuelsson & Kaga, 2008; UNESCO, 2007, 2008). The schooling and literacy education of the girl citizen-reader must ensure access and "allow for the active, free, and meaningful participation, contribution, and enjoyment of civil, economic, social, cultural and political development" (UNESCO/UNICEF, 2007, pp. 10–11). The emphasis throughout several years of UNESCO documents has been on the notion that the schooling and literacy of the girl citizen-reader must allow for active participation and equal participation with her male counterparts in a broad spectrum of activities in the public sphere (Samuelsson & Kaga, 2008; UNESCO, 2000a, 2000b, 2005a, 2005b).

The liberalism that underlies the UNESCO documents offers a powerful tool in securing equality and fairness for the girl citizen-reader to secure her universal global citizenship and her right to education and literacy. It can also be seen to threaten the difference of the *girl* citizen-reader, since she is to become like her brothers in opportunity and participation particularly in the public sphere, with the same citizenship identity. An alternative, especially for those girls and young women who are, or will be engaged primarily in the private sphere would be to valorize, honor or rename citizenship within the private sphere in more powerful ways. This is not a position evident in the documents, with one odd and interesting exception: in the positioning of the female teacher (Harper & Dunkerly, 2010; UNESCO, 2002, 2006). The work of the female teacher is named as follows:

> Women teachers provide new and different role models for girls—especially those in rural and conservative communities. They point to possibilities for women to be active outside the home and to be agents in community development. They play key roles in educating and socializing children beyond gender stereotypes, and so are crucial agents of change.
>
> *(UNESCO, 2006, p. 5)*

Here as a role model, the female teacher is to model the public sphere activity as an agent in the community outside the home, proving by example and instruction an alternative gender education, "beyond gender stereotypes." Although working with children (private sphere), but found in the public sphere she is a powerful and "crucial agent of change." However, although powerful, the female elementary school teacher is viewed as the medium or a role model through which her girl students will find their citizenship. Her public involvement is framed such as to render her activities as legitimate and natural by framing her public involvement as a service to her charges, rather than simply as an active citizen which effectively realigns her back into the private sphere.

This framing of the public work of the female primary teacher, as powerful and crucial as it might be deemed, means that the female teacher who operates in the public sphere to claim her own rights and citizenship, rather than in the interests of her charges, would be seen as strange, inappropriate, and perhaps as oddly unfeminine. Despite the effort made in the UNESCO documents to provide a powerful public citizenship for the female teacher (UNESCO, 2006) she is quickly rewrapped back within the private sphere, demonstrating how dominant the private/public alignment of gendered citizenship is and how difficult it continues to be to imagine and name women's citizenship outside of the private sphere.

Nonetheless, UNESCO's emphasis on literacy education as a universal human right lends critical importance to the work of female teachers in educating the girl citizen-reader. The education of the girl citizen-reader becomes a right, not a luxury, regardless of the particular economic, societal and cultural boundaries or circumstances of the girl herself or the nation-state.

The USAID Documents

In the USAID documents there is a strong focus on citizenship as an economic identity and the role of education in securing human capital for economic security and national productivity. USAID documents emphasize the importance of investing in educational opportunities in general, and for girls in particular. Moreover, they cite research that finds that each year of schooling "increases individual output by 4–7 percent, and countries that improve literacy rates by 20–30 percent have seen increases in gross domestic product (GDP) of 8–16 percent (Basic Education Coalition, 2004). In regard to girls' education, USAID's document, "Education from a Gender Equality Perspective" reports:

> When girls go to school, they tend to delay marriage, have fewer but healthier children, and contribute more to family income and national productivity. In fact, educating girls quite possibly yields a higher rate of return than any other investment available in the developing world.
>
> *(USAID, 2008, p. 1)*

In addition to these gains in human capital as an economic argument, USAID documents also revealed an organization that takes into consideration the local needs and practices that support or hinder education. While still couched in a context of supply and demand, the document, *Educating Girls: A Map to Contextual Analysis* (USAID, 2000) provides a framework for analyzing a given locale's policy along a matrix that takes into consideration not only legal and economic influences, but also cultural and societal norms and practices that influence girls' educational outcomes. Both the public and private spheres of the girl-citizen reader's life are at least considered. Many USAID documents also supported and reiterated UNESCO/UNICEF goals, most notably Education for All and other human-rights initiatives that move beyond a strictly economics-based public-sphere focus in considering the roles occupied by girls and women in both public and private. In USAID-funded education programs in Sudan, for example, programs have been designed to combat gender-related issues (private sphere) that contribute to a high illiteracy rate and low basic education completion rate for girls by providing scholarships (public sphere) and supporting the implementation of a gender-sensitive curriculum (USAID, 2005).

However, what constituted legitimate literacy education in the majority of USAID documents consisted largely of transplanted United States policy (e.g. *No Child Left Behind; Reading First*) into widely differing local sites through the Center for Excellence in Teacher Training (CETT) an initiative of the G.W. Bush administration and initially funded through, and now partnered with, USAID. Although materials available related to CETT spoke to the important role local teachers have in educating local children, the main focus of instruction was on an imported literacy curriculum favoring U.S. instructional practices supported by corporate partners in the United States, such as Scholastic, Ford Motor Company, DHL Global Delivery, and aluminum manufacturer ALCOA. CETT and USAID see these corporate partnerships as invaluable and mutually beneficial.

While the increase of literacy to the participating nations in Latin America and the Caribbean are no doubt mutually advantageous to both the individual and the nation-state, it is imperative to ask whose literacies and what identities for girls and women are being privileged and for what purpose. We must also ask "in our educational institution, what (and whose) view of the world are we giving to our students? Who is benefiting? Who is harmed? What knowledge of the world is absent, subjugated, disqualified" (Foucault, 1979, p. 135)? In this example, it appears that to be a good citizen of one's home country; to be a girl citizen-reader means being subjugated to U.S. educational policy and practices that are in turn supplying "a stronger more competitive workforce" to U.S.-based companies, regardless of the situated realities, values, and practices of students' culture, knowledge, and locality. Thus, local knowledge and identities especially as they relate to the private sphere of citizenship are neither honored nor seen as legitimate global participation for the girl citizen-reader, or for that matter, her male counterpart. Aligning literacy education primarily with economic participation and equating economic participation in the public sphere with national or global citizenship limits the citizenship of the girl citizen-reader. Furthermore, we suggest that this rather myopic scope and purpose for literacy and citizenship does not allow for the global/cosmopolitan sensibilities, and literacy skills and knowledge needed in forwarding the interests and development of the girl citizen-reader beyond the boundaries of her nation-state, except perhaps to serve the global economic interest of the sponsoring nation or companies/agencies.

Implications for Literacy Education

Although nearly all of the documents from both sources acknowledged the potential and the problems facing girls' literacy education, our analysis indicated that neither international source offered a specific naming of global citizenship. Nor did they seem to recognize the benefits of educating outside the figurative and literal boundaries of the nation-state. Indeed, the *girl citizen-reader* remains to a large extent defined within national boundaries and interests, particularly in terms of American policy and economic interests within the USAID documents.

By comparison, the UNESCO documents did position education and literacy as a universal human right—a right often denied girls in many countries. Even within a more global framework, the UNESCO documents still confined the girl citizen-reader within the boundaries of the nation-state rather than as a global citizen capable of reading in multiplicities globally. Across and within sites we were disappointed that there was not more of an emphasis on global citizenship. At the same time, we were surprised by the nature of citizenship defined so obviously within the public/private sphere.

What is called for, then, are literacy practices that emphasize global citizenship rather than one bound and defined by the nation-state. Specifically, we see the girl citizen-reader as in need of the following if she is to fully recognize global citizenship. She will require the assurance of equity in opportunity and participation with males in the public sphere. Given the strong support for the Education for All initiative in general and literacy education in particular across documents, we feel that this is an indicator of the potential for equality in global citizenship. In addition to equity in the public sphere, more work is needed to legitimize and strengthen the recognition and the role of private sphere citizenship. Moreover, the use and promotion of critical literacy practices (Bean & Moni, 2003; Morrell, 2008; Stevens & Bean, 2007) should be widely implemented in order to allow the girl citizen-reader to challenge the discursive rendering of gender. We see this use of critical literacy as needing to be informed by a feminist pedagogy that moves beyond that of liberal discourse (Cherland & Harper, 2007). In addition to examining national, international and supranational documents, we see sites of young adult popular culture, especially global young adult literature, as being implicated in the political sphere, and thus in need of further and future investigation (Bean & Harper, 2006). It is in these sites where the girl citizen-reader as well as her male counterpart are creating their own voices, informed by various expressions of identity and agency. Literacy educators in the U.S. and in other nations as well, can hopefully begin to use this discourse to promote the importance of the work they do and the need to insure access to quality literacy education for all students locally, nationally, and internationally that can in turn be used in all three contexts simultaneously and with fluidity. In recognizing the importance of the public and private sphere in education and in global citizenship, we argue that the work of literacy educators transcends national interests while creating a space for the girl citizen-reader to move beyond the borders of her nation-state and into the discourse of a global society.

References

Apple, M., Kenway, J., & Singh, M. (2005). *Globalizing education: Policies, pedagogies, & politics.* New York: Peter Lang.

Arnot, M. and Dillabough, J. (2000). (Eds.) *Challenging democracy: International perspectives on gender, education and citizenship*. London: Routledge Falmer.

Banks, J.A. (2004). *Diversity and citizenship education: Global perspectives*. San Francisco: Jossey-Bass.

Basic Education Coalition (2004). *Teach a child – transform a nation*. Washington, DC: Basic Education Coalition.

Bean, T.W. & Harper, H.J (2006). Exploring notions of freedom in and through young adult literature. *Journal of Adolescent and Adult Literacy 50*(2), 96–104.

Bean, T.W. & Moni, K. (2003). Developing students' critical literacy: Exploring identity construction in young adult fiction. *Journal of Adolescent and Adult Literacy 46*, 638–648.

Beck, U. (2002). The cosmopolitan society and its enemies. *Theory, culture & society, 19*(1–2), 25–44.

Benhabib, S. (1995). From identity politics to social feminism: A plea for the nineties, *Philosophy of Education*, 22–36.

Benhabib, S. (2006). *Another cosmopolitanism*. Oxford: Oxford University Press.

Cherland M.R. & Harper, H.J. (2007). *Advocacy research in literacy education: Seeking higher ground*. Mahwah, NJ: Lawrence Erlbaum Associates.

Chesterfield, R., Enge, K., & Martinez-Enge, P. (2001).*Girls education and crises*. Washington, DC: United States Agency for International Development.

Dillabough, J. (2000). In M. Arnot & J. Dillabough (Eds.) *Challenging Democracy: International Perspectives on Gender, Education and Citizenship*, pp. 155–176. London: Routledge Falmer.

Edwards, R. & Usher, R. (2000/2008). *Globalisation and pedagogy: Space, place, and identity*. New York: Routledge.

Fairclough, N. (2000). *Language and power* (2nd ed.). New York: Longman.

Foucault, M.(1979). *The History of Sexuality, Volume 1: An Introduction*, London: Penguin.

Foucault, M. (1980). *Power/Knowledge*. New York: Pantheon.

Foucault, M. (1991) 'Governmentality', trans. Rosi Braidotti and revised by Colin Gordon. In Graham Burchell, Colin Gordon and Peter Miller (Eds.) *The Foucault effect: Studies in governmentality*, pp. 87–104. Chicago: University of Chicago Press.

Foucault, M. (2000). *The essential works of Foucault* (Vol. 3, Power). New York: New Press.

Goldstein, T. (2007). Educating world teachers for cosmopolitan classrooms and schools. *Asia Pacific Journal of Education, 27* (2), 131–155.

Harper, H. & Dunkerly, J. (2010) Educating the world: Teachers and their work as defined by the United Nations Educational, Scientific and Cultural Organization (UNESCO) *Current Issues in Comparative Education, 4*, 56–65.

Harper, H., Bean, T.W., & Dunkerly, J. (2011). Cosmopolitanism, globalization and the field of adolescent literacy. *Canadian International Education Journal. Comparative and International Education Society of Canada*, 1–13.

Johnson, H. (2000). "To stand up and say something": "Girls only" literature circles at the middle level. *New Advocate, 13*(4), 375–389.

Kenway, J. with Langmead, D. (2000). Fast capitalism, fast feminism and some fast food for thought. In Ali, S., Coate, K., & Goro, W. (Eds.) *Global feminist politics: Identities in a changing World*, pp. 154–176. London: Routledge.

Luke, A. (2002). Curriculum, ethics, metanarrative: Teaching and learning beyond the nation. *Curriculum Perspectives 22*(1), 49–55.

Luke, A. (2004). Teaching after the market: From commodity to cosmopolitanism. *Teachers College Record, 106*(7), 1422–1443.

Morrell, E. (2008). *Critical literacy and urban youth: Pedagogies of access, dissent and liberation*. New York: Routledge.

Samuelsson, I. & Kaga, Y. (2008), *The contribution of early childhood education to a sustainable society*. Paris: UNESCO

Smith, S.A. (2000) Talking about "real stuff": Explorations of agency and romance in an all-girls book club. *Language Arts, 78*(1), 30–38.

Stevens, L.P. & Bean, T.W. (2007). *Critical literacy: Context, research and practice in the K–12 classroom*. Thousand Oaks, CA: Sage.

Summers, L. (1992). Investing in *all* the people. Policy Research Working Paper 905. Washington, DC: World Bank.

Tierney, R. (2006). Global/cultural teachers creating possibilities: Reading worlds, reading selves, and learning to teach. *Pedagogies: An International Journal, 1*(1), 77–87.

Tomasevski, K. (2003). *Education denied: Costs and remedies*. London: Zed Books.

Twomey, S. (2007). Reading "woman": Book club pedagogies and the literary imagination. *Journal of Adolescent & Adult Literacy, 50*(5), 398–407

UNESCO (1997) *Adult Education. The Hamburg Declaration: Agenda for the Future* CONFINTEA V, Hamburg: UNESCO Institute for Education. In: http://www.unesco.org/education/uie/documentation/confintea_5.shtml

UNESCO (2000a). *Final report. World Education Forum* (Dakar, Senegal, 26–29 April 2000). Paris: UNESCO.

UNESCO (2000b). *The Dakar Framework for Action: Education for All: Meeting our collective commitment*. World Education Forum, Dakar, Senegal, 26–29 April 2000. Paris: UNESCO.

UNESCO (2002). *A statistical profile of the teaching profession*. Paris: UNESCO

UNESCO/ILO (2003). *Committee of Experts on the Application of Recommendations Concerning Teaching Personnel*. Paris: UNESCO.

UNESCO (2005a). *Promotion of a global partnership for the UN decade of education for sustainable development: The international implementation scheme in brief*. Paris: UNESCO.

UNESCO (2005b). *Guidelines for Quality Provision in Cross-border Higher Education*. Paris: UNESCO.

UNESCO (2006). *The impact of women teachers on girls' education: Advocacy brief*. Bangkok: UNESCO.

UNESCO/UNICEF (2007). *A human rights-based approach to education: A framework for the realization of children's right to education and rights in education*. Paris/New York: United Nations Educational, Scientific and Cultural Organization & United Nations Children's Fund.

UNESCO (2008). Inclusive Education: International Conference on Education, 48th Session, Geneva, November, 2008.

USAID (2000). *Educating girls: A map for contextual analysis*. Washington, DC: USAID.

USAID (2005). *Improving lives through learning*. Washington, DC: USAID.

USAID (2005). *Meeting the global challenge: Progress in education 2005*. Washington, DC: USAID.

USAID (2007). *Gender equality in education: A dynamic framework*. Washington, DC: USAID.

USAID (2008). *Education from a gender equality perspective*. Washington, DC: USAID.

van Dijk, T.A. (1999). Critical discourse analysis and conversation analysis. *Discourse and Society, 10*(4), 459–460.

Walkerdine, V. & Lucey, H. (1989). *Democracy in the kitchen? Regulating mothers and socialising daughters*. London: Virago.

13

WHO WILL "SAVE THE BOYS"?

(Re)Examining a Panic for Underachieving Boys

Michael D. Kehler

In this chapter, I discuss what has quickly become known as the "boy crisis" in education. This rhetoric positions boys as the newly disadvantaged, particularly at the juncture of literacy and achievement levels in schools. In this chapter I examine how a growing panic about "the boys" is framed, defined, and connected to current practices intended to increase literacy achievement levels specifically among boys. I begin by providing a historical background to the now common reference to the boy crisis in education. While locating the broader rhetorical and policy-related response to underachieving boys, I critique provincial Ministry of Education directives in Ontario, Canada to "help the boys" and question how boys' underachievement levels are framed through school documents. I argue for a more nuanced national and international response, one that does not collapse and flatten *all* boys as the "newly disadvantaged". I conclude by questioning the re-inscription of normative masculinity and the limitations stemming from strategies that perpetuate and legitimize a "boys will be boys" position.

A Closer Look at the "Moral Panic" about Boys in Education

The rhetoric dominating much media and public attention among parents and educators has recently witnessed a dramatic shift, positioning underachieving boys as victims in a feminized world (Jacobs, 2008; Rowan et al., 2002; Titus, 2004). Alloway (2000) explains that the current round of debates in education are fuelled by a "crisis rhetoric about schooling outcomes for boys [that have] somehow transmuted into deep-seated moral panic centering on masculinity-at-risk. Concern about boys' school performance transfigured into concern about their performance of masculinity" (p. 334).

Alarmist terms calling for "help" and "saving the boys" have been freely cast about to suggest there is a crisis of masculinity. This "crisis" or emerging "moral panic," however, is not new. What is new is the way the term is being revived in current debates in education. Griffin (2000) for example, reminds us that the term "moral panic" emerged in the 1970s in relation to media representations of white, working-class men and gang wars between the Rockers and the Mods in seaside towns in the United Kingdom. In the UK, similar to Australia, Canada, and the United States, Francis (2006) explained that the debate about boys' literacy underachievement levels is not new, but admittedly is spreading among the nations represented by the Organization for Economic Co-operation and Development (OECD). It is worth mentioning that in the UK, Francis (2006) traced the debate back to the mid 1990s when the claims about boys' underachievement made headlines. At that time, feminists in the UK were already fully engaged in a critique of the moral panic about boys' underachievement in the media and education policy. Significant work had already begun by feminist scholars in the UK (e.g., Epstein et al., 1998) but, according to Francis, had waned under the pressure of anti-feminist attacks.

The latest debate to capture media and public attention which has ultimately led many to name boys as the "newly disadvantaged," has emerged from the *Messages from PISA 2000* report by the OECD (2004), which summarized the findings of learning outcomes for OECD countries. The difficulty, however, remains in the interpretation of the data presented and the failure by some to question or interrogate the statistics. In particular, there has been an absence of critical examination of the data cited indicating differences between boys' and girls' performance levels in reading and writing. The findings are useful as a platform for further understanding how issues of gender and literacy are framed, and, how the ideological terrain in education, along with political maneuvering, takes place to move the concerns about boys and achievement levels to the status of a moral panic or crisis (see Martino & Kehler, 2007).

Jacobs (2008) reminded us that the crisis in adolescent literacy is not new though admittedly "the language of crisis has successfully brought the needs of adolescent readers to the fore politically, theoretically and practically" (p. 11) after remaining in relative obscurity for some thirty years. Responding to boys' literacy in Canada and the US, Froese-Germain (2006) similarly cautioned against the strong rhetoric driving the debate and instead suggested a more textured examination of the debate that calls for "disaggregating data on boys, by race, social class, geography (urban vs. rural), and other factors. In short, the crisis is not as dire as the media hyperbole might suggest. Froese-Germain argued that it is misguided and mistaken to assume all boys are in trouble because "in the same way that not all girls are excelling, not all boys are doing poorly" (2006, p. 148; for further discussion see Cappon, 2011). It is striking and disturbing, however, that amidst this rhetoric of crisis and moral panic, the Ontario Ministry of Education positions boys as part of a group of "at risk" individuals. In *Realizing the Promise of*

Diversity: Ontario's Equity and Inclusive Education Strategy document, the authors explained:

> Recent immigrants, children from low-income families, Aboriginal students, boys, and students with special education needs are just some of the groups that may be at risk of lower achievement. To improve outcomes for students at risk, all partners must work to identify and remove barriers and must actively seek to create the conditions needed for student success. In an increasingly diverse Ontario, that means ensuring that all of our students are engaged, included, and respected, and that they see themselves reflected in their learning environment.
>
> *(MOE, 2009a, p. 5)*

This framing of boys as disadvantaged or invisible in the curriculum and learning environment denies and erases any sense of context and history of privilege occupied by boys, specifically white, middle-class boys. Instead, as Keddie and Mills (2008) argued, boys are being re-cast as an equity group in the gender and schooling debate through a competing victims' discourse that removes equity concerns from broader relations of gender and power. This approach effectively removes compounding factors of race and class from the equation and "deflects attention away from issues of genuine disadvantage especially in relation to marginalized groups of girls" (Keddie, 2010, p. 1). To parallel boys with other marginalized groups whose histories are not comparable thus raises serious questions about the positioning and response to "save the boys" in the current literacy debate.

The resurgence in the apparent "crisis of masculinity" (for elaboration see Connell, 1995) and "moral panic" about boys is about more than simply academic achievement. It is as much about how the debate is being framed through particular ideological lenses as it is about what in particular is mobilizing a response in such a rapid fashion. Connell (1995) makes a useful distinction between the concept of crisis tendencies and the colloquial sense in which people speak of a "crisis of masculinity." As a theoretical term "*crisis* presupposes a coherent system of some kind, which is destroyed or restored by the outcome of the crisis." Masculinity however, is not a system in that sense according to Connell (1995). As Connell argued, "it is, rather, a configuration of practice within a system of gender relations" (p. 84). She explains that "we cannot logically speak of the crisis of a configuration; rather we might speak of its disruption or its transformation" (p. 84). Along this line, it is more accurate to speak of "a crisis of a gender order as a whole and of its tendencies toward crisis" (p. 84).

In his account of the "boy turn" Weaver-Hightower outlined the way that some education research has shifted toward boys and schooling and away from the inequities that characterized concerns for girls in education in the mid 1980s. His analysis usefully situates the evolution of the debates within the literature by suggesting a range of categories that highlight how concerns have been framed and moved forward in various intellectual landscapes. (For further discussion see Jones and Myhill, 2004; Keddie, 2010).

Reading Beyond a Populist Discourse

In report after report—from Canada to the United States to Australia and the United Kingdom—the media has painted boys as the "victims" of an education system that has been pushed too far by radical feminists seeking to support girls at the expense of boys' achievement and success. Francis (2006) argued that this resurgence in popularity of a poor boy discourse effectively situates boys as "defeated and damaged" (p. 189). Absent from much of the debate is any discussion or acknowledgment of the how and for whom race and class intersects in the ongoing discussion and policy decisions responding to concerns for boys and schooling. In her analysis of 11- to 14-year-old London boys, Ann Phoenix (2004), for example, argued that the current debate to help boys relies on a powerful neoliberal discourse that normalizes and homogenizes boys as a coherent and undifferentiated group. In her study she describes "boys' struggles to present themselves as properly masculine within the social changes characteristic of a neoliberal discourse of individualism".

The panic about boys emerges from several discourse communities. In their collection of essays, Epstein et al. (1998) provided a rich discussion of the tensions and underlying factors mobilizing the debate about boys. In brief, three camps of thought about boys and how to respond to them presently dominate the field of education. "Pity the poor boys," as Kenway (1995) described it, starts from the position that boys are under attack and their masculinity is threatened. Boys are under siege; women and specifically feminists are apt to take boys' natural power away and leave them vulnerable and weak. As such, women are at fault for the failure of boys. The "failing schools, failing boys" discourse centers on the institutional level and draws heavily on school improvements, school effectiveness, and standards-based rhetoric. Within this framework issues are defined by concerns for competition.

The more broadly accepted and widely adopted discourse is that "boys will be boys." Its broad-based appeal is not surprising given the long history associated with a bio-determinist position that assumes behaviors are genetically linked. The binaristic notion that boys are aggressive and girls are passive, for example, further homogenizes boys as a coherent and undifferentiated group. The continued attention to boys' underachievement is driven by what Keddie and Mills (2008) described as a "discourse of entitlement" in which schools adopt boy-friendly remedies that only further privilege the masculine while at the same time contributing to a polarization of boys and girls as learners. A commonsense acceptance and repositioning of boys as being asked to be unmanly is adopted in a way that regularly invokes naturalized notions of masculinity on the basis of biological difference which is then scripted onto learning strategies.

The Positioning of Boys' Literacy Underachievement: From Policy to Practice

In central Canada, the Ontario Ministry of Education has produced and widely disseminated two major documents that directly address boys' literacy underachievement. The strategies and direction proposed in these documents are indicative of a particular gender-based literacy reform in elementary and secondary schools at a provincial level. In the first of two guides, *Me Read? No Way! A practical guide to improving boys' literacy skills* (MOE, 2004), intended for teachers and administrators, the Ministry provides a set of thirteen teaching "Strategies for Success" intended to contribute to a "stimulating and engaging learning environment for both boys and girls" (p. 2) with a set of strategies that "represent practices that will enhance the learning environment for both boys and girls" (p. 4). The follow-up publication, *Me Read? And How! Ontario teachers report on how to improve boys' literacy skills* (MOE, 2008), dovetailed from the first with a direct focus on boys. In this second document, the authors are clear that its development and publication offers teaching strategies and resources specifically "designed for boys." The "findings" presented in this document emerge from the Ministry of Education (http://www.edu.gov.on.ca/eng/curriculum/report.html) which has funded and supported teachers in adopting specific strategies to respond to boys' literacy achievement. The focus is on "changing teaching practices related to boys' literacy achievement" not on improving or changing pedagogical practices that support *all* student achievement. Instead, the Ministry has adopted a gender-specific reform that reifies and valorizes a very narrow and limiting understanding of masculinity and what it means to be a boy on the basis of specific masculine stereotypes that feed into boys' literacy practices (MOE, 2009a, p. 9).

The Ministry publications were widely distributed in print and available online for teachers and Faculties of Education across Ontario. And while both documents address boys' literacy, the first document claims that the practices provided are useful for engaging both boys and girls. The second document was targeted specifically at boys at the elementary and secondary level, as well as parents, who are "concerned about their sons' literacy skill and who may wish to advocate for their use in their sons' school." And while each document claims that the strategies are "designed for all students, including girls" (MOE, 2009a, p. 4) the second document remains wedded to providing the "best pathway" for boys. The report shared strategies and practices developed by teachers who:

> revised their instructional practices; and deepened their joy in teaching *boys*. Through their thoughtful and dedicated pursuit of the inquiry work, teachers not only furthered their understanding of *boys* and their learning

needs and styles but also experienced insights into the strategies that work best with *boys* and the specific aspects of schooling that can impede their learning.

(MOE, 2009a, p. 4, emphasis added)

It is clear that the focus, the strategies, and the practices that teachers developed and implemented were designed with a gender-specific reform approach grounded in an ideological framework positioning boys and girls as distinctly separate learners. The follow-up document was intended for use on several levels; one of which is for advocacy and change on the backs of parents who are encouraged to bring to bear the specific literacy strategies promoted by the Ministry. Parents were encouraged to draw on the document when raising concerns for boys' literacy achievement. The second document (*Me Read? And How!*) reaches beyond teachers in its scope by drawing on parents to not only accept a particular ideological position of boys as specific types of learners but to engage parents as advocates for their sons, and to mobilize parents through a Ministry initiative. The earlier document (*Me read? No Way!*) was "designed for browsing" (MOE, 2004, p. 2). There is a clear shift in how the Ministry sees these documents operating in schools and specifically literacy classrooms. The Ministry focus has moved from a "guide of rich resources" to a document that is directed and funded by the Ontario Ministry of Education on the basis of team proposals to conduct inquiries into strategies for improving boys' literacy skills. The agenda for promoting a specific gender-based reform approach in boys' literacy is further evident in the later publication which is premised on the position that:

As evidence continues to show that many boys are not flourishing in the school environment, educators believe that there needs to be more precise attention paid to, and continuing, in-depth investigation conducted into, the issue of boys' literacy.

(MOE, 2009a, p. 6)

Rather than broadening boys' repertoires of ways for understanding and learning, the current boy-friendly strategies and practices to improve achievement levels reflect a limiting approach that narrows and ultimately crystallizes traditional notions of masculinity and femininity through gender-based reforms.

A review of the number of instances the terms "boys" and "girls" were used in these documents reveals a striking polarizing effect in the way instruction and strategies are directed. In the *Me Read? No Way!* document, there were 263 instances of "boys", 46 instances of "girls" and 14 instances when "boys and girls" are captured together. The *Me read? And How!* document produced 540 instances of "boys", 70 instances of "girls" and 27 instances in which "boys and girl" were coupled together. This document does not provide strategies for teaching *all* students, but rather a specific population of students, namely boys. Although the authors claim that the literacy strategies might be used for both boys and girls, the number of times that boys and girls are referred to together is minimal. The incidence of girls as a term unto itself is often used in polarizing and restrictive ways that pit one sex *against and in opposition* to the other. Taken from *Me read? No Way!* (MOE, 2004) the following examples illustrate how boys and girls are framed as diametrically opposed and coherent categories:

- "Boys typically score lower than girls" (p. 4)
- "Boys read less than girls" (p. 6)
- "Boys value reading as an activity less than girls do" (p. 6)
- "Girls are not able to connect directly with subjects but a boy can only connect with the subject via the teacher" (p. 46).

Moving beyond the problematic of international panics for "poor boys"

Concerns for boys and achievement levels are woven into a seamless and predictable pre-existing set of gendered understandings based in bio-determinist assumptions that evoke a widespread reform to ensure that, as Titus (2004) points out, "the prevailing social order is maintained" (p. 159). Boys will be restored to their rightful and historically contextualized place of superiority where according to the Ministry, they have vanished and can no longer "see themselves reflected in their learning environment" (MOE, 2009a, p. 5) and moreover, according to Ontario literacy initiatives to help boys, they "face barriers to learning" and resources are required to "*help* boost boys' reading skills" (p. 14, emphasis added).

Rather than respond with fear driven by a panic to help boys improve achievement levels, we need to better ask how and why some boys continue to resist, to struggle to understand, to struggle to embrace and embody multiple forms of masculinities, ones that would support, promote and encourage a rich and broad repertoire for learning in schools.

Implications for Literacy Education

The ramifications of policy practices, resources, guides, and teaching strategies that are based on bio-determinist arguments to the exclusion of social understandings of what it means to be a boy are considerable. Without first interrogating masculinity and its place within schools we are doomed as educators to maintain, perpetuate, and reinforce harmful and even damaging ways of being boys through literacy practices that directly and indirectly allow boys to be boys, at any cost. We must critically question the underachievement debate and the oversimplification of its current rendering in relation to literacy education. There are implications for both boys and girls. As Jones and Myhill (2004) explained,

> Teachers know what underachievement looks like, it looks like a boy who is bright, but bored. Girls, by contrast, are not bored: they are keen and hardworking . . . Underachieving boys have . . . taken on an identity, a set of teaching strategies, and a whole branch of research all to themselves . . . [while] the underachieving girl remains a shadowy vague figure, almost invisible.
>
> *(Jones and Myhill, 2004, p. 560)*

Educators and teachers need to look broadly rather than narrowly at the scope of the concerns pointed at boys as victims. In the closing pages of *Exploring the "Boy Crisis" in Education* (Cappon, 2011), the authors cautioned educators against generalizations about all boys and all girls. It is to our peril as teachers and educators if we do not acknowledge and act upon the fact that there is simply more variation of achievement levels within groups of boys and within groups of girls than across groups of boys and girls on achievement scores. Amidst the crisis rhetoric that prevails nationally and internationally, we are reminded, that after thousands of studies examining the contributions of various factors affecting student achievement, "gender differences account for an impact of only 0.12 of a standard deviation" (see Hattie, 2009 in Cappon, 2011). Interestingly—or surprisingly—this fact is rarely reported. We are faced, instead with a boys as disadvantaged paradigm that "has gained an unprecedented truth status" on the basis of "reductionist comparative measures of gender performance [that has] re-ignited constructions of boys as victims" (Keddie, 2010, p. 2).

Policy and practice intervention in literacy education should be aimed at raising "participation and achievement levels generally, and/or targeting disaggregated sub-populations facing particular obstacles, barriers or difficulties" (Cappon, 2011, p. 49). Sub-groups of boys and girls then are a population where educators might provide specific and intentional support that addresses the performance scores of the sub-groups such as boys and girls who are a part of the larger more general population. The binaristic logic that currently dominates most responses to save the boys and improve underachievement levels of boys is unhelpful and indeed counterproductive for ensuring all students learn well.

References

Alloway, N. (2000) Exploring boys' literacy performance at school: Incorporating and transcending gender. *Contemporary Issues in Early Childhood, 1*(3), 333–337.

Cappon, P. (2011). Exploring the "boy crisis" in education. Ottawa: Canadian Council on Learning.

Connell, R.W. (1995). *Masculinities*. Berkeley: University of California Press.

Epstein, D., Ellwood, J., Hey, V., & Maw, J. (1998). School boy frictions: Feminism and "failing" boys. In D. Epstein, J. Elwood, V. Hey, & J. Maw (Eds.), *"Failing boys": Issues in gender and achievement* (pp. 3–18). Buckingham, UK: Open University Press.

Francis, B. (2006). Heroes or zeroes? The discursive positioning of "underachieving boys" in English neo-liberal education policy. *Journal of Education Policy, 21*(2), 187–200.

Francis, B. & Skelton, C. (2005). *Reassessing gender and achievement: Questioning contemporary key debates.* Abingdon, UK: Routledge.

Froese-Germain, B. (2006). Educating boys: Tempering rhetoric with research. *McGill Journal of Education, 41*(2), 145–154.

Griffin, C. (2000). Discourses of crisis and loss: Analyzing the "boys' underachievement" debate. *Journal of Youth Studies, 3*(2), 167–188.

Hattie, J. (2009). *Visible learning: A synthesis of over 800 meta-analyses relating to achievement.* Abingdon, UK: Routledge.

Jacobs, V. (2008). Adolescent literacy: Putting the crisis in context. *Harvard Educational Review, 78*(1), 7–39.

Jones, S. and D. Myhill (2004). "Troublesome boys" and "compliant girls": Gender identity and perceptions of achievement and underachievement. *British Journal of Sociology of Education. 25*(5), 547–561.

Keddie, A. (2010). Feminist struggles to mobilize progressive spaces within the "boy-turn" in gender equity and schooling reform. *Gender and Education,* (iFirst), 1–16.

Keddie, A. & M. Mills (2008). Disrupting masculinised spaces: Teachers working for gender justice. *Research Papers in Education,* (iFirst), 1–14.

Kehler, M.D. (2010). Boys, books and homophobia: Exploring the practices and policies of masculinities. *McGill Journal of Education, 45*(3), 351–370.

Kenway, J. (1995). Masculinities in schools: Under siege, on the defensive and under reconstruction? *Discourse: Studies in the cultural politics of education, 16*(1), 59–79.

Lingard, B., Martino, W., & Mills, M. (2009). *Boys and schooling: Beyond structural reform.* Basingstoke, England: Palgrave Macmillan.

Macleans (2005, October 31). "The age of the wuss", "The sad slump of North American manhood". Cover.

Martino, W. & Kehler, M.D. (2007). Gender-based literacy reform: A question of challenging or recuperating gender binaries. *Canadian Journal of Education, 30*(2), 406–431.

Martino, W., Kehler M.D., & Weaver-Hightower, M. (2009) (Eds.), *Schooling masculinities: Beyond recuperative masculinity politics in boys' education.* New York: Routledge.

(MOE) Ontario Ministry of Education (2004). *Me read? No way! A practical guide to improving boys' literacy.* Toronto: Queen's Printer for Ontario.

(MOE) Ontario Ministry of Education (2008). *Me read? And how! Ontario teachers report on how to improve boys' literacy skills.* Toronto: Queen's Printer for Ontario.

(MOE) Ontario Ministry of Education (2009a). *The road ahead: Boys' literacy teacher inquiry project 2005–2008.* Toronto: Queen's Printer for Ontario.

(MOE) Ontario Ministry of Education (2009b). *Ontario's equity and inclusive education strategy.* Toronto: Queen's Printer for Ontario. Retrieved September 7, 2010, from http://cal2.edu.gov.on.ca/april2009/EquityEducationStrategy.pdf

Organization for Economic Co-operation and Development (OECD). (2004). *Messages from PISA 2000.* Paris: OECD Publications.

Phoenix, A. (2004). Neoliberalism and masculinity: Racialization and the contradictions of schooling for 11 to 14-year-olds. *Youth & Society, 36 ,* 227–246.

Rowan, L., M. Knobel, C. Bigum, & C. Lankshear (2002). *Boys, literacies and schooling: The dangerous territories of gender-based literacy reform.* Buckingham, UK: Open University Press.

Titus, J. (2004). Boy trouble: Rhetorical framing of boys' underachievement. *Discourse: Studies in the Cultural Politics of Education, 25*(2), 145–169.

Weaver-Hightower, M. (2003). The "boy turn" in research on gender and education. *Review of Educational Research, 73*, 471–498.

14

INVENTING MASCULINITY

Young Black Males, Literacy, and Tears

David E. Kirkland

Black men don't always cry in the dark (Baisden, 2001). Sometimes, young Black men spill pain on paper and write with tears as monuments to their literate craft. From Jay-Z (2001) who in "Song Cry" admits, "I can't see 'em comin down my eyes / So I gotta make this song cry," to Tupac (1994) who confesses in "So Many Tears," "Though I walk through the valley of death / I shed so many tears (if I should die before I wake) / Please God walk with me (grab a nigga and take me to Heaven)," the face of Black masculinity is almost fully revised in the practice of Black masculine literacy (Kirkland & Jackson, 2009). Both Jay-Z and Tupac in their plays on tears mark a disruption in the dominant, media-produced discourse on the Black male as hyper-masculine, subhuman, and cold as ice (Cose, 2002). Both songs place pause in the ether, complicating our common understandings of who Black males are and who they are supposed to be. They further raise questions about the contents of Black male writings and the character of the Black male and his transfixed and fluid realities. If, then, the artifact of tears works to complicate how Black males are imagined, how might tears also help us to complicate the Black male as literate?

A Trope of Tears: Black Male Literate Traditions, Organic Pheminist Thought, and Tyrek

Jay-Z and Tupac aren't the first Black males to comment on the world using the trope of tears. Black male writers have historically used this trope to express a pain common to most Black folk but peculiar to the Black man. Moreover, within this *border masculinity* (the masculinity that sits between hegemonic masculinity and its opposite), new practices of literacy are enabled, and some of our most celebrated Black male writers have crafted counter-masculine narratives that use the ink of the tear. For example, Paul Laurence Dunbar (1993) uses tears to illustrate the passions of Black folk in his poems titled "Sympathy" (1893, 1899), where he sheds light on the "tear another's tears bring forth". For Dunbar, tears articulated the powerful testimony pronounced in wet eyes while pivoting toward the transient, still living story of the oppressed. His writings marked the scene of Black eyes crying, relenting something akin to scripture. "I know why the caged bird sings," in Dunbar's second "Sympathy" (1899), is eulogy—a statement that is compassionately honest, engendering the brevity and rectitude of the shortest verse in the Christian Bible: like Black men, "Jesus wept."

Curiously, the synonym of such tears in the Black male literate tradition is far from grief yet something closer to struggle. This was the case for James Weldon Johnson (Johnson & Johnson, 1928) who in his poem "Lift Every Voice and Sing" speaks of a people who "have come over a way that with tears has been watered." This same people, through swallow cries and resounding seas, emerge socially baptized on the hills of some "list'ning skies," perhaps cleansed in the agony of Langston Hughes's (1994) "rivers that run deep" though hidden in the promises of the "God of our silent tears." From Dunbar to Johnson to Hughes and on to Jay-Z and Tupac, Black males have made the teardrop vogue. Because of writers such as them, the tear has emerged as a Black masculine literacy artifact. In this tradition, some Black men even today sketch tears on skin (e.g., the teardrop tattoo on the faces of rappers such as Lil' Wayne and Game) to reinvent Black masculinity. For such writers, the tear is significant as it makes room for a revision of *hegemonic masculinity* (Butler, 1993) so fully realized that the composition of the crying Black man feels less a social aberration than a gendered invention. Thus, the tear acts not only as symbol, but also as space that invites possibility for Black men to write with weeping and in the lineage of a historical lamentation that places pens in the hands of modern Black male psalmists, such as a young Black male I studied, named Tyrek.

I met Tyrek in the fall of 2008 while conducting an ethnography of urban youth literacies in Brooklyn, NY. He was only 14 years old then, tall and slender, and one of the few Black male poets on the NYC youth slam team. Tyrek was acutely aware of the elements of writing and much of how he viewed the world was a response to or a reflection of how he viewed himself through the eyes of his mother and sisters. According to Tyrek, "My mom and my sisters mean the world to me." He would later explain, "I write poetry for them. A lot of my poems be about them."

Tyrek's view of the world through his mother and sisters' eyes suggested a feminism that helped me to examine the presence of tears in his poetry. In other places, I have called this feminism *organic pheminism* (Kirkland, 2010) to distinguish it from other academic varieties. Unlike academic feminisms, I suggest that organic pheminism is not the product of theoretical debate, but rather something more fluid, relative, and situated, emerging from our participation in the world and through our interactions with (other) females. According to Spillers (1994),

"The African-American male has been touched . . . by the *mother, handed* by her in ways that he cannot escape, and in ways that the white American male is allowed to temporize by a fatherly reprieve" (p. 80, italics in the original). It is by this "handed"-ness and those female touchings that we, both women and men, come to see, through the shadows of this world and through the eyes of its women, the women we know and care about and for, and who also occupy our lives, the under-explained existences of individuals whom many of us too easily overlook.

The Black female perspective is vital for understanding the Black male, both as human and as writer. According to Spillers:

> the black American male embodies the only American community of males which has had the specific occasion to learn *who* the female is within itself, the infant child who bears the life against the could-be fateful gamble, against the odds of pulverization and murder, including her own. It is the heritage of the *mother* that the African-American male must regain as an aspect of his own personhood—the power of "yes" to the "female" within.
>
> *(Spillers, 1994, p. 80, italics in the original)*

The lens of the "female within" presents in clear shade the dialectics of the common spectacle, where though one feels limited to the constructs of dominant ideologies and their hegemonic impulses, one never is truly or fully prisoner to their seemingly fixed paradigms of thought and desire, behavior and response.

I use the ph spelling for pheminism to further distinguish organic pheminism from perspectives, or feminisms, belonging to other traditions, seeking to locate pheminism in the public sphere, particularly hip hop culture, where ph spellings for words with /f/ sounds signal semantic alterations as well as cultural specificity. My point is to point to a deviation in history and in meaning, to offer a new idea or lens for framing literate phenomena that is pupilled by new focal points to trace the word (and thus the idea), to bear witness to a past and its experiences as seen in the echo of the literate utterance. It was through this lens, an organic pheminist lens, that I approached Tyrek's two poems and the complex meanings related to their production.

"Endless Seas": Exploring the Role of Tears in the Production of Border Masculinities in Tyrek's Two Poems

Two of Tyrek poems illustrate well the tear-troped tradition of other Black male writers. He titled the first poem "Cry No More."

1   Little boy
2   I see you settled in your agony
3   Drowning in oceans of want

4   Wanting more than your failed eyes can see
5   Standing on dreams in the footprints of Kings
6   Cheeks wet with the rain of urgency
7   Little boy
8   I see you swimming in puddles of hopeless sorrow
9   Suffering to walk on the waters that dampen your mother's feet
10   You dive deep in rivers that torrent and bleed
11   And your sisters' tears clothe you
12   Little boy
13   I see you . . .
14   You must be me
15   Because I, like you, am drowning in the tears of my own endless
     seas

Though the term *tears* is only mentioned twice in the poem, the trope of tears is resident throughout the text. Tyrek signals this trope in his title, "Cry No More." By line 3, he compares tears to "oceans of want." In line 6, he introduces "cheeks wet with the rain of urgency," and by line 8, the little (Black) boy being discussed is "swimming in puddles of hopeless sorrow." By line 10, he is diving "deep in rivers that torrent and bleed." Each image characterizes the depth of tears specific to the Black male experience, which, for Tyrek, lives in the waters that "dampen your mother's feet."

While Tyrek's poem exemplifies the trope of tears through much of the imagery in the text, his actual mentioning of tears moves readers beyond trope to social commentary. In line 11, Tyrek imagines the little boy's "sisters' tears" as clothing and later in line 15, "as hiw own endless seas." In each instance, tears smother the Black masculine body and metaphorically operationalize oppressive structures that cover/clothe and possess/drown Black men. While the tears are not always his—and in at least one instance they belong to his sisters—tears as metaphor for imprisonment (see also Dunbar's second poem "Sympathy") semantically inverts the symbol, linking it to the new Jim Crow. According to Kennedy (2001), one in three Black men experience some aspect of the prison industrial complex—either currently incarcerated, formerly incarcerated, or on their way to being incarcerated. The other two-thirds of Black males who escape the vicious cycle of state-sanctioned bondage linger under threat of incarceration and the justified paranoia that comes with it.

As many people have associated tears with weakness and have gendered it in opposition to masculinity, Tyrek's poem uses the tear to revise normalized notions of masculinity, reinventing it in a border space between what's expected of a male and what's expected of a female, a third space where gender is not so much neutral as it is shared. In this way, Tyrek occupies a similar space as Black male writers such as Antwone Fisher, who in his poem "Who Will Cry for the Little Boy?" constructs Black masculinity in tears, if not in drag. Tyrek's little boy, echoing

Fisher, wears the tears of his sisters as a symbol that bares the historical veracity of the Black male body. Here, the Black male body is revealed through its experiences with the female within and the female around. This brush with femininity does not situate Tyrek, as writer or as Black male, away from a heteronormative performance of literacy (Smith & Wilhelm, 2002). Rather, it reconstructs him through those organic pheminist leanings that he gains from having a mother and two sisters who share in his agony over the subjugation of Black bodies.

We see in Tyrek's poem the lingering consequences of patriarchy. According to Tyrek, "I carry my mother's tears so that she does not have to cry. I hate to see a woman cry, especially my mother." In his explanation, Tyrek signals at least two important points significant to his appropriation of the tear as both literacy artifact and as border masculine act. At one level, he receives his tears from more than the historical traditions of Black males but understands tears from his mother's experience. This understanding expresses, in a very human way love and yet occupies the hegemonic masculine space of savior/protector. Then, the second point significant to Tyrek's appropriation of the tear is the way he masculinizes it. He doesn't admit to carrying tears for himself or his fallen brothers, but for his mother. In this instance, the male pose is reified by the event of carrying (as in care) for, particularly, a woman as though she cannot carry tears (care) for herself. In this instance, Tyrek doesn't so much revise hegemonic masculinity as he reinforces it. Yet one can distinguish this embrace of masculinity from other forms. His is, nonetheless, an affectual act, an act of "love." Although it can be construed as oppressive in this particular form, Tyrek's act of love is constructed not in spite of women but because of them and in the blind shades of the heart.

For Tyrek,

> I want to be different than the other men I know. [*Laughs.*] I don't know no man who is willing to just cry. Even though we do, none of the men I know will just be free with crying. But if you bring up his momma . . . man . . . [*Pauses. Laughs.*] he'll yell, scream, cry, shout . . . I think it is okay to cry for our mothers and sisters and other women we love because we love them. And all the Black men I know love they momma. They do. That relationship, that one, gives us permission to cry and still be a man.

I must point out that though he discussed this relationship, the relationship between Black men and their mothers in relation to tears, Tyrek's explanation privileged not a revision but only a pause in our broader conception of masculinity. As a Black male, he didn't necessarily feel free to cry. For him, tears would be justified and in this case related to "mothers and sisters and other women we love because we love them." Further, while he was in the process of remaking masculinity through tears, Tyrek was also affirming hegemonic masculinity. It's not so much, then, that Tyrek's use of tears gave him reprieve from the ideological grips of hegemonic masculinity. Rather, his use of tears offered him an alternative space to write within, which allowed Tyrek to invite a softer form of himself into his text where he could invent, with his pen, ways to be "different than the other men."

Tyrek's other poem, titled "Tears of another," also illustrates this invention.

1   I am still crying
2   These are not my tears
3   But they belong to me
4   And have for many years

"Tears of another" also works in the literate traditions of other Black males (see line 4). Like Dunbar, Tyrek uses rhetorical paradox to reimagine masculinity as a trait of history as much as a trait of man. However by line 3, he claims the "tears of another" while admitting, "These are not my tears." His paradox of ownership admits to a particular type of agency/responsibility, though it has not graduated to the arrogance and ambivalence that typifies Cose's (2002) "envy of the world." Instead, Tyrek's use of tears to portend agency tends toward the affective, submitting to the social and gendered imagination, while inventing and revising masculinity as pertaining to realities that do not always fit the stable products of manhood.

His image is imagination—the evidence of invention. According to Appadurai:

> The image, the imagined, the imaginary—these are all terms which direct us to something critical and new in global cultural processes: the imagination as a social practice. No longer mere fantasy (opium for the masses whose real work is elsewhere), no longer simple escape (from a world defined principally by more concrete purposes and structures), no longer elite pastime (thus not relevant to the lives of ordinary people) and no longer mere contemplation (irrelevant for new forms of desire and subjectivity), the imagination has become an organized field of social practices . . . a form of negotiation between sites of agency ("individuals") and globally defined fields of possibility.
>
> (Appadurai 1993, p. 274)

Seen in the scape of written tears, Black manhood moves beyond villainy to desire in Tyrek's poem. Similar to Appadurai's rethinking of imagination, its invention of manhood is social practice, and the tear, itself, works as a social literacy tool, recomposing the Black male body to establish a kind of new flesh capable of new meaning. In this way, the tear beyond mere comment or trope becomes a fluid literacy artifact of the Black male body that permits a hearing of an unspoken humanity that brings the Black male as literate subject (as opposed to literate object) beyond his sympathies and yet closer to knowing himself and his possibilities for acting within a liberated space of compassion and sentiment.

Implication for Literacy Theory and Education

I have argued in other places that much of the so-called Black male literacy crisis is made up (Kirkland, 2011a). The other parts are man-made. What's made up suggests that Black males lack literacy, failing to consider literacy in the light of Lave and Wenger (1991), who suggest that individuals develop as a matter of environment and within affinity groups, ritualized events/activities, and complex processes of interaction situated within sites of value. For them, development is fluid and progressive. The novice participants located on the edges of practice and in the process of being a part of (as opposed to apart from) and doing acts of collective being through time and engagement become more central participants in their communities of practice.

Likewise, Gutierrez and Rogoff (2003) suggest that development is guided by culture, or the practices that shape belief, understanding, identity, etc. specific to a given affinity group's ways of acting. Extending Moll's (1990) notion of "funds of knowledge," they describe "repertoires of practice," which fundamentally shift knowledge from the static state of knowing to the active state of doing (as in practicing). In each of these examples, capacity is based in potential and located in the social scripts that individuals come to master and more fluently perform. Learning is seen as shared, as a human trait defined only by the borders of particular and situated human experiences, events, expressions of thought, and so on. Indeed, Scribner and Cole (1981) construct their insights on literacies in this tradition, suggesting that literacy development is not only culturally constituted, it is culturally enabled.

The literacy crisis as self-made results from our misunderstanding and hopeless labelings of Black males as deficient. In this way, many Black males endure classrooms constructed in opposition to who they are, have been, or hope to be. There have been countless data evincing Black male opposition to school literacy on the basis of literacy being presented as the providence of females and Whites. There is also a good deal of evidence suggesting that teachers of literacy know little about how to enhance literacy among Black males and who also feel that the literacies Black males practice aren't worthy of classroom space. Moreover, in recent years, scholars have begun to explore a set of literacy myths, in particular the myth of the illiterate Black male thereby adding texture to the scholarship. In so doing, many have concluded that Black males, in fact, practice literacy but in ways that endorse two obvious polarities—epicene masculinities (Young, 2007) and hyper masculinities (Cose, 2002). The epicene Black literate narrative tends to queer the Black male literate act as homoerotic, therefore positing alternative masculinities in league with non-dominant sexualities. However, Tyrek's poems and the tear-troped Black male tradition in which he writes suggest that there are multiple masculinities at work in tears, invented by Black males—queer and straight that contribute new content and new motivations for Black males who read and write.

The hyper-masculine Black male performances, by contrast, have long endured in the literature and have left us with shadowy and loose figurations of meaning, locating the Black male reader and writer in a sort of homogeneous vacuum. This view of him erases sexual and social complexity, and plays on the thematics of violence, hypersexuality, machismo, and so on to orchestrate a stable but unreliable fiction of who Black men are. Hence, the items of curricula it produces characteristically distill into aggressive and shallow logics that ultimately debase the human sensitivities of individuals, such as Tyrek, into caricatures that play empty on our most limiting stereotypes.

Let me be fair here. I am not exempt from this type of error. In some of my early work (Kirkland, 2006) and unfortunately in some of my most recent work (Kirkland, 2011b), I, too, have cast Black males in almost-monolithic nodes. I, too, have been guilty of oversimplifying the relationship among hyper-masculine expressions found in Black male literacy artifacts and their conversations about literacy and the actual alternative artifacts that place them closer to the borders of masculinity. However, when one reads the world with limited insight, one's vision is equally limited. Yet, through the writings of Tyrek, I have been able to extend my own vision to see a new cultural script on Black masculinity. Thus, I have examined Tyrek's use of tears to penetrate the hegemonic masculine imagination that besmirches the impassive image of some venerable man. In their relationship with Black men, tears articulate a new cultural script where Black manhood is written as an axiological figuration of something that (re)presents the physical endurings of the Black male body.

Still, in many ways tears are not understood as part of the public performance of Black masculinity. Yet, in moments of deepest sincerity, Black men, such as Tyrek, have long cried and have used tears to create a border space where Black males write with feeling and emotion. Then, in a fine organic pheminist sense, young Black men too pick up, or appropriate, if you will, the various available identities—including femininities—to foster masculinities that are useful in affective moments (hooks, 2004). If taken as real, the act of inventing masculinities suggests that Black males, and certainly all men, are not prisoners to historically bound and oppressively legislated legacies of maleness or confined to problematic modules for being or becoming men. It also means that what seems stable in terms of how we know Black men and what we think we know of them as readers and writers, may be as unstable as the term masculinity itself, which too shifts in moments of complexity when traditional scripts are no longer useful.

References

Appadurai, A. (1993). Disjuncture and difference in the global cultural economy. In B. Robbins (Ed.), *The phantom public sphere* (pp. 269–295). Minneapolis: University of Minnesota Press.

Baisden, M. (2001). *Men cry in the dark*. Chicago: Sal Val.

Butler, J. (1993). *Bodies that matter: On the discursive limits of "sex."* New York: Routledge.

Carter, S., Gibbs, D., Johnson, R., & Smith, J. (2001). Song Cry. On *The Blueprint*. New York: Roc-A-Fella Def Jam.

Cose, E. (2002). *The envy of the world: On being a Black man in America.* New York: Washington Square Press.

Dunbar, P.L. (1993). *The collected poetry of Paul Laurence Dunbar.* Charlottesville: University Press of Virginia.

Gutierrez, K.D. & Rogoff, B. (2003). Cultural ways of learning: Individual traits or repertoires of practice. *Educational Researcher, 32*(5), 19–25.

hooks, b. (2004). *We real cool: Black men and masculinity.* London: Routledge.

Hughes, L. (1994). The Negro speaks of rivers *The collected poems of Langston Hughes.* New York: Alfred A. Knopf.

Johnson, J.W. & Johnson, J.R. (1928). *Lift every voice and sing.* New York: Edward B. Marks Music.

Kennedy, R. (2001). Racial trends in the administration of criminal justice. In N.J. Smelser, W.J. Wilson & F. Mitchell (Eds.), *America becoming: Racial trends and their consequences* (Vol. 2, pp. 1–20). Washington, DC: National Academy Press.

Kirkland, D.E. (2006). *The boys in the hood: Exploring literacy in the lives of six urban adolescent Black males.* Unpublished dissertation, Michigan State University, East Lansing.

Kirkland, D.E. (2010). 4 Colored girls who considered suicide/when social networking was enuf: A Black feminist perspective on literacy online. In D.E. Alvermann (Ed.), *Adolescents' online literacies: Connecting classrooms, digital media, and popular culture* (pp. 71–90). New York: Peter Lang.

Kirkland, D.E. (2011a). Books like clothes: Engaging young Black men with reading. *Journal of Adolescent & Adult Literacy, 55*(3), 199–208.

Kirkland, D.E. (2011b). "Something to brag about": Black males, literacy, and teacher education. In A. Ball (Ed.), *Studying diversity in teaching and teacher education* (Vol. 3, pp. 183–200). Washington, DC: AERA.

Kirkland, D.E. & Jackson, A. (2009). "We real cool": Toward a theory of Black masculine literacies. *Reading Research Quarterly, 44*(3), 278–297.

Lave, J. & Wenger, E. (1991). *Situated learning: Legitimate peripheral participation.* Cambridge: Cambridge University Press.

Moll, L. (1990). *Vygotsky and education: Instructional implications and applications of sociohistorical psychology* (Introduction). Cambridge: Cambridge University Press.

Scribner, S. & Cole, M. (1981). *The psychology of literacy* (Chapter 14, The practice of literacy, pp. 234–260). Cambridge, MA: Harvard University Press.

Shakur, T., Jacobs, G., Walker, R., Baker, E., & Wonder, S. (1994). So many tears. On *Me against the world.* Los Angeles: Soundcastle Studios.

Smith, M.W. & Wilhelm, J.D. (2002). *"Reading don't fix no Chevys": Literacy in the lives of young men* Portmouth, NH: Heinemann.

Spillers, H. (1994). Mama's baby, papa's maybe: An American grammar book. In A. Mitchell (Ed.), *Within the circle: An anthology of African American literary criticism from the Harlem Renaissance to the present* (pp. 454–481). Durham, NC: Duke University Press.

Young, V.A. (2007). *Your average Nigga: Performing race, literacy, and masculinity.* Detroit: Wayne State University Press.

15

GENDERED SUBJECTIVITIES IN ONLINE SPACES

The Significance of Genderqueer Youth Writing Practices in a Global Time

Jennifer C. Ingrey

Rethinking genderqueer youth subjectivities in online spaces in a context of globalization has strong implications for literacy education. In this chapter, I attempt to reflect on these intertwining fields, gender subjectivities (i.e. the performance and expression of gender identity) and online literacy through an examination of one conversational thread (i.e. a sequence of comments posted online by multiple users) in the teen forum on Laura's Playground (laurasplayground.com), a website dedicated to transgender individuals.

Using Stromquist's (2002) definition, globalization shapes both a "neoliberal development model that emphasizes the market and a technological revolution that has increased the ubiquity and speed of production and information technologies" (p. 6). Online literacy practices of genderqueer youth can be analyzed using these two arms of globalization: neoliberal education that seeks to measure and manage an individual's literacy outcomes; and the impact of the Internet on writing practices and gender identity. A project seeking to do justice to gender nonconforming/genderqueer youth in education rejects a neoliberalist framework because it cannot account for a diverse gendered population nor justify how genderqueer youth may need extra attention. It is through an analysis of youth's online writing made possible by the technological advances of globalization that we can gain insight into their experiences to deconstruct neoliberalism's "normative versions of the idealized gendered economic subject" (Davies & Saltmarsh, 2007, p. 8). Davies and Saltmarsh (2007) explain that "being gendered shapes individual interest and engagement in literate practices. Literate practices in turn shape the ways in which one becomes gendered" (p. 8). Thus, through participation and recognizability, gender and literacy are connected. Literate practices within online communities, especially those that serve a transgender youth population, depend upon a certain level of participation which is also requisite for being gendered. And being gendered and being literate require a kind of recognizability, replete with markers and codes, within a community (Davies & Saltmarsh, 2007). These markers or codes of literacy are the very linguistic elements of writing (i.e. words, grammar, punctuation); in gender, markers and/or codes are comprised of modes of expression, or how one walks, talks, gestures, and dresses that communicate a certain gender identity.

Luke and Carrington (2004) explored the effects of globalization on literacy education through their metaphor of "globalised 'flows' to explain the impact of new media, new cultures and new economies on children's identities and developments" (p. 53). These "flows" characterize globalization in terms of how "bodies and capital, information and image" (p. 54) can move so easily across political and geographical borders which contests the binary of local and global, or micro and macro. These flows constitute the "glocal," the merging of the global and the local. The authors argue the institution of schooling, originally meant to create the modern individual literate in print and possessing an encyclopedic knowledge, as well as of a monocultural identity, will now have trouble accounting for the borderless flows in this globalized age. They wish to push the notion of literacy into a consideration of how students are positioned, and position themselves, in the "glocal," both online and in physical space (p. 53). Literacy education that incorporates a view of students living within a "glocalized" world can also begin to deconstruct the way these youth have been normalized, and their learning practices rendered static. The framework of Luke and Carrington and others working within globalization in education acknowledges the challenges that genderqueer youth and online learning pose to literacy education.

Literary Practices Online

I take up Driver's (2005) initiative to study the online activities of queer youth because in her words, "youth make use of the Internet as a realm to try out, play with, and perform their identities and desires through provisional combinations of images, words, and narratives" (p. 111). This "play" and "trying out," however, does not revert to the postmodernist view of the disembodied individual; as I will discuss, gendered individuals are as much physically and emotionally affected by their online as their offline activity.

MacIntosh and Bryson (2008) argue that researchers and educators alike must "be paying attention" to the online activity of sexual minority youth (in their case, queer youth on MySpace) primarily to get a glimpse into the "community-building and the shifting terms of belonging and identification . . . [which are] the mechanisms of their sociality" (p. 138). These social networking sites are not devoid of the "rules" of social engagement; these authors argue against the utopia promised in the early days of the Internet as one where disembodied identities were entirely free to be remade. Rather, even queer identity is qualified by multiple and complex relationships and their interactions with(in) a community

(p. 139). Similarly, Leander and McKim (2003) argue that physical space is relevant, in relational terms (see McGregor, 2004; Soja, 1996), to research sites of online activity because participants "do not see their experiences online as remarkable or separated from their day-to-day lives" (p. 218). In offline material spaces, genderqueer youth must contend with the regulation of their gendered embodiment; online spaces offer a new, if not entirely free, possibility of being in part because they are disembodied and borderless.

In studying online and offline activities in distance education, Sanchez (1998) rejects a postmodern view of the Internet that divides the mind from the body and sees the individual as able to play out multiple versions of the self freely. He argues this mind/body split serves a neoliberalist agenda in two ways: one, because a disembodied mind does not take up physical space that an institution must own and maintain which allows class sizes (and therefore revenue) to expand beyond the spatial limits of the classroom; and two, this mind is also a passive receptacle to now receive information bits in a most cost-efficient way. Instead, Sanchez argues the mind is embodied because when one laughs out loud, or feels angry while reading certain texts, the body is very much implicated in online activity (p. 99). Paired with Foucault's (1982) work on power and knowledge, Sanchez's work informs how I see the individual as formed in and through power systems and discourse which makes a disembodied mind too simplistic and erroneous a concept. The ultimate danger of neoliberal online education, Sanchez (1998) warns, results in a "panoptical nightmare" (p. 101) where the individual is under constant surveillance and detection, thus threatening the freedom of students otherwise allowed to develop in out-of-school, unsupervised literacy practices. Following Sanchez's advice to check often how our bodies are affected by technologies, online activities of genderqueer youth can be examined for how their texts speak to an embodied experience of gender.

If online space is not devoid of embodied implications, then it is also not completely separated from rules of social engagement. The complexity of online individuals both disembodied and embodied can also be explained in Foucauldian terms where the individual is produced through power relations or what Foucault (1982) terms, disciplinary power. For Davies (2006), who reworks Judith Butler's "subject," agency is conditional, not ultimate, and acts in the form of the subject examining their conditions and subverting them in part (Davies, 2006, p. 426). Using these frameworks on the subject or the individual, we can see how genderqueer youth online are *contingent* subjects, conditional subjects, who navigate the twists and turns between agency and determinism. Youth can be thought of as embedded in these power structures, no matter which space (material or virtual) is inhabited.

What the discourse on the subject can point to is a form of social imaginary; through Butler's (1990) gendered subject, who is capable of resistance, the imaginary of gender justice is possible because this subject conceptually marks out the limits of possibility to expand what is intelligible (p. 40). I draw on several gender theorists who think about the imaginary, or the possibility of gender justice. Martino (2012) embraces a *transgender imaginary* that distinguishes gender from biological sex in favor of a "non-hegemonic, non-normative" system of gender. This imaginary requires researchers and educators to value the knowledge and experience from gender nonconforming individuals. Further, the imaginary, according to Martino and Rezai-Rashti (2011), is the alternative to the hetero-normative and heterosexist constraints in dominant discourse about gender.

Similarly, Renold and Ringrose (2011) use the concept of *fantasy* as a space of agency to understand how youth both negotiate and resist gender norms and heteronormative discourses. And Connell's (2009) form of imaginary promotes gender democratization over an abolishment of gender strata, in the way that we cannot ignore gender but seek to find justice within the codes of gender expression and identity. I apply the imaginary to genderqueer youth to allow for a rethinking of gender, one that allows for a just treatment of all gendered bodies, regardless of how much they may or may not conform.

Examining Sites of Possibility

I am examining a part of the teen forum in Laura's Playground (http://www. lauras-playground.com/index.htm), which is named, "A Transgender Umbrella Resource Community Online." According to the homepage, it is "an [*sic*] multi-platform TG/TS support site which includes, friends, articles, advice column, FAQ's, live chat, forums, online games and horoscopes." Alexa, a website dedicated to figuring and reporting statistics for online activity, notes the average user age of "Laura's Playground" is between 45 and 54, but the teen forum is designed specifically to provide a safe space for teens. At the beginning of each post, each member is identified by an image, or a tag or name of their choosing (recommended not to be their real name for safety purposes). The site includes a section to indicate their interests, country, and "gender status" which honors self-naming in the sense that users are the sole authors of their online identity: how they choose to identify and present themselves to the world is completely under their control, as far as these identifiers are concerned. The site also has a multi-language option on the homepage, promises to update regularly, and claims to be the only site with youth suicide prevention moderators online who are trained in the same way as those moderating suicide prevention hotlines.

In this vein of suicide prevention, the site serves as a reactive to current socio-cultural trends of transgender-as-victim induced by transphobia; and in some ways, it also pathologizes the trans teen experience as ultimately imbued with violence and in need of psychological counseling. Access to texts written by trans or genderqueer adolescents is limited, however, especially in the public domain. It is with some qualification that I cite the thread that I selected to share here, but I choose to view it as productive for its contribution to knowledge of gendered subjectivities. As Driver (2005) noted, online texts can be "highly articulate, spontaneous" and an "integral part of queer [or even genderqueer] youth representation" (p. 112). This forum can be thought to be the type of "grassroots creative cultural practice" (Driver, 2007, p. 210) that Driver insists is necessary to reshape methodologies examining queer (or genderqueer) youth experiences and knowledge.

My examination was bound by one thread of posts in the teen forum started by Jesse0319, self-named as an 18-year-old senior in a north-midwestern high school. This thread is titled, "RLE at School—FtM/Jesse Style," started February 21, 2012, and inspired by another member's post, FemtoKitten, from January 17, 2012, on her MtF (male to female transition) experiences at school. The thread is relevant for literacy education because the initial post was framed as a short story, contained headers, was written chronologically and thematically, and had ensuing comments from readers; and primarily, the context was about one's RLE (real-life experience necessary for transitioning gender dysphoric individuals) in school.

I acted as a "lurker" researcher (Leander and McKim, 2003), or "guest" indicated when reading a post online, which had impact on my ability to access information. Because I was not a member of the site, I could not interact with members by posting responses, nor could I verify online identities and match them to "real life" identities. I heeded Richman's (2007) advice to employ researcher reflexivity when studying cybercultures, considering the "role of memory, [and] the location of the outsider" (p. 183). I emphasize the *partiality* of this knowledge (Kumashiro, 2000) and I chose to follow Leander and McKim's (2003) methodological direction that tracing stories, or metaphors, is a legitimate way to access the "spatial-identity-literacy practices of adolescents" (p. 232).

Online Writing from Genderqueer Individuals, Jesse and FemtoKitten

Jesse0319 wrote his story about living as a boy/man in high school as part of his transition. He traced his journey through various subthemes that I identified as self-naming through symbols, effects on embodied reality, and issues of safety and community. The details about self-naming speak to agency, which is necessary when thinking about how to do justice to genderqueer youth's knowledge about their experiences. To take up this latter theme is to frame what is also more easily understood about these sorts of websites: they are about forming a community, a transnational one at that, albeit from the global North (the users in this thread alone are from the USA, the UK, Canada and Australia), that is otherwise impossible in the physical local spaces of the users. This community offers emotional and crisis support (as indicated on the homepage of the website), and through promised constant surveillance to maintain a safe environment—to "keep the BADDIES out" (from Elizabeth K., Member, posted 17 May, 2011, 9:30 pm)—it answers the "dual need for public voice and protection from regulation and surveillance [which] is especially crucial for marginalized youth" (Driver, 2005, p. 111).

The website also acts as both a prompt and a prop to users to form a community of support within their own home environment. For example, Jesse0319 wrote that he continued to find supportive teachers within his own school to educate them about transgender RLE. He also inspired Kael147 (another member who responded to Jesse0319's post) to develop a plan for coming out at his own office. Jesse0319 responded to Kael147's plans by posting: "Wow, thanks for the encouragement . . . And I'm glad to unwittingly help, Kael."

I discuss only one topic in examining these exchanges—the embodiment/disembodiment complex. I followed Driver's (2007) recommendation to look for moments of discord, those that interrupt "dominant ideologies and powers" (p. 309). This embodiment/disembodiment complex interrupts dominant narratives about transgenderism—how the body gets transformed monopolizes popular thinking about what it means to be a transgendered person. How that physical transformation gets played out online, in a supposedly disembodied space, is precisely the dichotomy I wanted to investigate because the performativity of gender is about "an identity tenuously constituted in time, instituted in an exterior space through . . . bodily gestures, movements, and styles of various kinds" (Butler, 1990, p. 179). How the physical stuff of gender, the *matter* (Butler, 1993)—which are, as Butler explains, really the "effect[s] of gender" (1990, p. 179)—begin to matter in online spaces is part of the conundrum of studying online practices.

Jesse0319 borrowed FemtoKitten's move that using a token or a symbol to represent one's preferred name/identity is necessary to prove "that I was me when at school". For FemtoKitten, as an MTF, it was a pink backpack. For Jesse0319, undergoing an FTM RLE, it was a key chain "with MY name on it" and it "helped tremendously". For both users, writing about how they wish to signify their preferred identity visually at school was both supportive and inspiring. The form of writing a short story speaks to a wider audience with hopefully equally inspiring results. How these youth are somewhat free, contingent agents (Davies, 2006) to write their own identity online is also implicated in their very real physical experience at school which is regulated by gender-normative practices. They are limited by what is possible, normal gender markers (i.e. the *pink* of the backpack), but then use that possibility to ease their own transition, to stand as constant and quiet reminders of who they are and want to be.

The issue of embodiment emerges again in another scenario: Jesse0319 tried to untangle the ethical and practical problems of room sharing on an upcoming class trip. He envisioned using that opportunity to come out, but he did not know where he and his body would fit. Before coming out as Jesse, the teacher would assign him a room with female students; only after coming out would this be an obvious problem. Jesse felt uncomfortable rooming with boys also because he still looks and sounds female. In a follow-up post, Jesse0319 wrote that he would be rooming with three girls he did not know which would, he claimed, "make it easier . . . to just say right off the bat, 'Hey, I'm trans . . . so . . . I'll sleep on the floor, and please don't parade around without clothes. Thank you.'" In the form of a narrative, Jesse0319 wrote his own future which although fraught with embodied implications, was performed as seamless on this virtual stage of the website. Embodiment in physical life is an embodiment performed online; or, a seemingly disembodied presence online is actually imbued with real-life embodiment, but gets a rehearsal or a try-out online: it is a form of embodied play, as Driver (2005) found in her studies of queer youth homepages, and a moment of fantasy (Renold & Ringrose, 2011). The rehearsal takes on the qualities of imagination which is "potentially transformative" because it allows "youth to envision alternative gender relations" (Driver, 2006, p. 244) that are less harmful than those in their school lives.

FemtoKitten's initial post of her at-school RLE was peppered with references to her embodied self. She began by writing, "I am sitting on my bed (and listening to Owl City) wearing a pink t-shirt and with kitten pajama bottoms". It was necessary for her to paint that image to present herself in this way as an apparent typical 17-year-old female, but with force and power. The kitten, as indicated in her online moniker, is another symbol of female power and a symptom of her agency. Both FemtoKitten and Jesse0319 performed their gendered subjectivity literally through the texts about embodiment, and in Butler's (1990) terms of *gender performativity*, which explain that the body comes into a gendered being through "a stylized repetition of acts" (p. 179). The trans teens used the space of this online forum by "staking out new terms and territories of identification and belonging" (Driver, 2006, p. 231), a growing practice of queer youth who are otherwise "isolated and individualized within their everyday lifeworlds" (p. 230).

Implications for Literacy Education

Although I did not literally dialogue with these youth online in this forum, I hope to contribute to an overarching project that seeks to value this sort of identity writing as literary practice and one that refuses to limit youth writing by neo-liberalist agendas of measurement, or heteronormative/gender-normative systems. Driver's (2007) fear that "discordant moments of speech that remain unintelligible according to social scientific categorizations" (p. 309) implies that future research must not do away with the unintelligible. That which does not make sense initially, or that which resists categorization, is precisely the kind of "unintelligible" form of writing to consider against the intelligible; in this case, writing from genderqueer youth operates as an "unintelligible" form of knowledge. Educators must ask why it does not fit, however, and how it reinforces the norm of gender (Butler, 1993). Otherwise, the only sort of information recognized will only contribute further to a hegemony of knowledge and prevent new understandings from emerging about how youth write their identity.

Davies and Saltmarsh (2007) noted that neoliberal education agendas depend upon a literacy program that constructs all children as possessing a monolithic identity in terms of learning styles (p. 8). These researchers argued that neoliberal education cannot account for diversity or unmeasurable moments of literate subjectivities that are a reality of the globalized world. Non-measurable literacy practice must be allowed in the classroom. It must be understood that literacy practices are intimately linked with an awareness of gender. Leander and Lovvorn (2006) argued, "understanding how engagement, agency, and identity involve particular displacements in space-time offers valuable insights for how literacy learning and instruction may be more optimally organized and designed" (p. 294).

In this way, the Internet, as a new classroom, may be thought of as a *heterotopic* space (Foucault & Miskowiec, 1986) or space that is connected but other than, outside the real, normalized space that offers even more possibilities for literacy education (Birr Moje, 2004). We can ask how the classroom (and so too the curriculum) remains relevant, or how it can be reconsidered while maintaining the value of these non-school literate practices without it turning into a "panoptical nightmare" in the neoliberalist regime of hyper-management and measurement (Sanchez, 1998). If we reject out-of-school literacy practices, we must consider how that can devalue in-school work, limiting students to explore their gendered subjecthood only elsewhere in unguided online forums when they are already at the point of crisis, and requiring suicide protection.

Online learning, although riddled with conceptual and practical troubles, still has implications for literacy education. Online activities do have value, they are relevant, and they are tied to the subjecthood of the user. Online practice in its shifting spatial and temporal borders allows genderqueer youth to create a community that helps them to understand and explore their gender expression (Driver, 2006). Taking Luke and Carrington's (2004) view that globalization creates flows that position and consequently exclude certain marginalized populations, we must ask how to engage genderqueer youth who are already among the excluded in pedagogy and curriculum through a consideration of their literary practices online. Tapping into the needs of this population by valuing what they are already doing is to make their processes of subjectivity and literacy more meaningful. To think within a social imaginary in a globalized time is to rethink the nature of literacy education altogether in the name of gender justice.

References

Alexa. Retrieved March 5, 2012, from http://www.alexa.com/siteinfo/lauras-play ground.com

Birr Moje, E. (2004). Powerful spaces: Tracing the out-of-school literacy spaces of Latino/a youth. In K.M. Leander & M. Sheehy (Eds.), *Spatializing literacy research and practice* (pp. 15–38). New York: Peter Lang.

Butler, J. (1990). *Gender trouble: Feminism and the subversion of identity*. New York: Routledge.

Butler, J. (1993). *Bodies that matter: On the discursive limits of "sex."* New York: Routledge.
Butler, J. (1995). Contingent foundations: Feminism and the question of "postmodernism."
In S. Benhabib, J. Butler, D. Cornell, & N. Fraser (Eds.), *Feminist contentions: A philosophical exchange,* (pp. 35–57). New York: Routledge.
Connell, R.W. (2009). *Gender.* Cambridge: Polity.
Davies, B. (2006). Subjectification: The relevance of Butler's analysis for education. *British Journal of Sociology of Education, 27*(4), 425–438.
Davies, B. & Saltmarsh, S. (2007). Gender economies: Literacy and the gendered production of neo-liberal subjectivities. *Gender and Education, 19*(1), 1–20.
Driver, S. (2005). Out, creative and questioning: Reflexive self-representations in queer youth homepages. *Canadian Woman Studies, 24*(2–3), 111–116.
Driver, S. (2006). Virtually queer youth communities of girls and birls: Dialogical spaces of identity work and desiring exchanges. In D. Buckingham & R. Willet, (Eds.), *Digital generations: Children, young people, and new media* (pp. 229–245). Mahwah, NJ: Lawrence Erlbaum Associates.
Driver, S. (2007). Beyond "straight" interpretations: Researching queer youth digital video. In A.L. Best (Ed.), *Representing youth: Methodological issues in critical youth studies* (pp. 304–324). New York: New York University Press.
Elizabeth K. (2011, May 17). Message posted to http://www.lauras-playground.com
FemtoKitten. (2012, January 17). Message posted to http://www.lauras-playground.com
Fornet, Betancourt, R., Becker, H., Gomez-Muller, A. & Gauthier, J.D. (1987). The ethic of care for the self as a practice of freedom: An interview with Michel Foucault on January 20, 1984. *Philosophy and Social Criticism, 12*, 112–131.
Foucault, M. (1980). *Power-knowledge: Selected interviews and other writings, 1972–1977.* (C. Gordon, L. Marshall, J. Mepham, & K. Soper, Trans., Colin Gordon, Ed.). Hassocks, UK: Harvester Press.
Foucault, M. (1982). Afterword: The subject and power. In H.L. Dreyfus & P. Rabinow (Eds.), *Michel Foucault: Beyond structuralism and hermeneutics.* Chicago: University of Chicago Press.
Foucault, M. & Miskowiec, J. (1986). Of other spaces. *Diacritics, 16*(1), 22–27.
Jesse0319. (2012, February 21). RLE at School – FtM/Jesse Style. Message posted to http://www.lauras-playground.com
Kumashiro, K. (2000). Toward a theory of anti-oppressive education. *Review of educational research, 70*(1), 25–53.
Leander, K.M. & Lovvorn, J.F. (2006). Literacy networks: Following the circulation of texts, bodies, and objects in the schooling and online gaming of one youth. *Cognition and Instruction, 24*(3), 291–340.
Leander, K.M. & McKim, K.K. (2003). Tracing the everyday "sitings" of adolescents on the internet: A strategic adaptation of ethnography across online and offline spaces. *Education, Communication and Information, 3*(2), 211–240.
Luke, A. & Carrington, V. (2004). Globalisation, literacy, curriculum practice. In T. Grainger (Ed.), *The RoutledgeFalmer reader in language and literacy* (pp. 52–65). New York: RoutledgeFalmer.
MacIntosh, L. & Bryson, M. (2008). Youth, MySpace, and the interstitial spaces of becoming and belonging. *Journal of LGBT Youth, 5*(1), 133–142.
Martino, W. (2012). In Greig, C. & Martino, W. (Eds.), *Canadian men and masculinities: Historical and contemporary perspectives* (Chapter 11: Queering masculinities as a basis for gender democratization: Toward embracing a transgender imaginary). Toronto: Canadian Scholars' Press/Women's Press.

Martino, W. & Rezai-Rashti, G. (2011). In *Gender, race, and the politics of role modeling* (Chapter 11: Conclusion: Towards a social imaginary beyond role modeling). New York: Routledge.

McGregor, J. (2004). Spatiality and the place of the material in schools. *Pedagogy, Culture and Society 12*(3), 347–371.

Renold, E. & Ringrose, J. (2008). Regulation and rupture: Mapping tween and teenage girls' resistance to the heterosexual matrix. *Feminist Theory, 9,* 313–338.

Renold, E. & Ringrose, J. (2011). Teen girls, working-class femininity and resistance: Retheorising fantasy and desire in educational contexts of heterosexualised violence. *International Journal of Inclusive Education,* doi:10.1080/13603116.2011.555099.

Richman, A. (2007). The outsider lurking online: Adults researching youth cybercultures. In A.L. Best (Ed.), *Representing youth: Methodological issues in critical youth studies* (pp. 182–202). New York: New York University Press.

Sanchez, R. (1998). Our bodies? Our selves? Questions about teaching in the MUD In T. Taylor & I. Ward (Eds.), *Literacy theory in the age of the internet* (pp. 93–106). New York: Columbia University Press.

Soja, E.W. (1996). *Thirdspace: Journeys to Los Angeles and other real-and-imagined places.* Malden, MA: Blackwell.

Stromquist, N. (2002). *Education in a globalized world: The connectivity of economic power, technology, and knowledge.* New York: Rowman & Littlefield.

INDEX

Page numbers in **bold** refer to figures

cultural resources 65
culturally responsive teaching 27
culture jamming 32
Cushman, Karen 17, 20
cyberflâneurs 75

Davies, B. 17, 140, 142, 147
democratization 44
design literacy 106
Dewey, R. 92
difference: advocacy 68–69, **69**;
  deconstructing 59; repression of 60
digital literacy **68**; advocacy 68–69, **69**;
  blogs and blogging 69; and body image
  66–67, **68**; data collection 65–66; and
  gender identity 64–72; and identity
  construction 70–71; and literacy
  education 71–72; rural communities
  91–92; as social practice 64–65; *see also*
  online practices
Dillabough, J. 111
discourse 76, 142
Disney 33–34, 36
disposable income, tweens 31
distros 54–55, 56–57
diversity 61
DIY or Don't We? 57
Do You Hear Me? (Franco) 27
documentary film 13–16
doing good 36–37
Donehower, K. 95
Double Dutch (Draper) 84
Draper, Sharon 84
dress 67, 74, 75, 76
Driver, S. 141, 143–144, 146
Duke University 97
Dunbar, Paul Laurence 132, 136
Dunn, A.E. 93
Dunn, R.A. 96, 98
"Dysfunctional Relationships" campaign
  15

economic participation, and literacy
  education 117
*Educating Girls: A Map to Contextual
  Analysis* (USAID) 116
education: and citizenship 112; feminized
  24; international agencies 112–113;
  male-domination 23; and masculinity
  23; resistance to 26
Education, U.S. Department of 93

Education for All initiative 113, 116, 118
"Education from a Gender Equality
  Perspective" (USAID) 116
embodiment 145–146
Empowered Youth Program (EYP) 77
empowerment 34, 35, 38, 61
enabling texts 27
engagement 72, 147; and allusion 6–7;
  community/work-based learning and
  8–10; contexts for 3–10; and ICT
  9–10; and language contexts 4; popular
  media and 4–7; through music 4–6; use
  of new media 4; video gaming
  107–108
entrepreneurship education 74–81;
  clothing website descriptions 77–78;
  clothing websites cultural modeling 78;
  data sources 77; and gendered
  discursive practices 74, 76, 81; and
  literacy education 80–81
epicene masculinity 137
Epstein, D., et al. 124
equal rights 96–97
ethnic identity 70
everyday identity 44
Exploring the "Boy Crisis" in Education
  (Cappon) 128

Facebook 44, 48, 58, **68**, **69**, 71, 72
Fadiman, A. 93
"Faith and Hope in the Feminist Political
  Novel for Children: A Materialist
  Feminist Analysis" (Hubler) 17
False Start 57
fan fiction 106
fantasy 136, 143
father-son relationships 14
female becoming 19
female citizenship 111–112
female detective novels 19
female touchings 133
female within, the 133
femininity: challenging traditional 20; and
  cool 25; negotiations 48–49; and social
  media 49; and zines 53–61
feminism 132–133; Marxist 18; material 20
feminist poststructuralism 56, 76
feminist sociology 56
Fennell, S. 97
Fine, M. 76
Fink, L. 93

Harper, H. 23
Harper, Helen 13, 37–38
hegemonic masculinity 27, 131, 132, 135
Heilman, E.E. 61
heterotopic space 147
Hicks, Deborah 97
Hip-Hop 4–6, 133
Hogg, C. 95
Hubler, Angela E. 17, 20
Hull, G.A. 45
human capital 25, 116
human rights 114–115, 116
Hush (Woodson) 84
hyper masculinity 137–138

"I Love to Give You Light" (song) 5, *5*
ICT, and engagement 9–10
idealized narratives 19
identity: anchorage 47; and citizenship
    115; and digital literacy 64–72; ethnic
    70; everyday 44; exploring 26–27;
    gender. *see* gender identity; language of
    70; and literacy 46; and literacy
    education 146–147; markers 44, 47;
    multiple 61; negotiations 48–49; online
    43–50; performance 23, 46–47; queer
    141–142; queer youth 141; and reading
    19; re-mixing 50; and self-love 59–60;
    transient 47; and video gaming 103
identity categories, problematized 76
identity writing 144–146, 146
identity-construction 65, 70–71
imaginary, the 136
imaginary worlds 17
immigrants 61; advocacy 68–69, **69**; body
    image 66–67, **68**; and digital literacy
    71; gender identity 64–72; and
    language 70; learning environment 72
independent learning 10
India 36
individualization thesis 44
information and communication
    technologies (ICTs) 75, 91, 96
interactivity 72
Internet, the 6, 58, 96, 141–142, 147;
    access 75, 93; Web 2.0 technologies
    44, 49–50, 54; *see also* social
    networking sites (SNSs)
interviews 13, 58
Invisible Children 15
invisibility, African American females 83

Jackson, Michael 32
Jacob (child soldier) 14
Jacobs, S. 92
Jacobs, V. 122
Jay-Z 131, 132
Johnson, James Weldon 132
Jones, S. 127–128

Kantor, Julie Silard 74
Keddie, A. 123, 124–125, 128
Kehily, M. 50
Kellner, Douglas 33
Kennedy, R. 133–136
Kenway, J. 75, 124
Ker-Bloom 57
Knobel, M. 102, 107
Kony, Joseph 13–16
Kony 2012 (YoutTube video) 13–16, 18
Krisher, Trudy 20

labor, sexual division 18
Lamb, Sharon 34
language: of identity 70; lack of neutrality
    113–114; and patriarchy 16; specialist
    105
language contexts 4; authentic 8–10;
    community/work-based learning and
    8–10
Lankshear, C. 102, 107
Lansberg, Michelle 18
Lapping, M.B. 95
late modernity 44, 50
Latin America 117
Laura's Playground
    (laurasplayground.com) 140, 143–146
Lave, J. 137
Leander, K.M. 142, 144, 147
learners' identities 71
learning environment 72
learning structures 6
learning styles 147
Lee, Lia 93
Let the Circle be Unbroken (Taylor) 16–17
liberation 17
"Lift Every Voice and Sing" (Johnson)
    132
literacy: and identity 46; out-of-school 56;
    re-conceptualization 64–65; as social
    practice 56; and video gaming
    101–108
literacy competence, development of 3–10

Taylor & Francis

eBooks
FOR LIBRARIES

ORDER YOUR
FREE 30 DAY
INSTITUTIONAL
TRIAL TODAY!

Over 23,000 eBook titles in the Humanities,
Social Sciences, STM and Law from some of the
world's leading imprints.

Choose from a range of subject packages or create your own!

Benefits for **you**

▶ Free MARC records
▶ COUNTER-compliant usage statistics
▶ Flexible purchase and pricing options

Benefits for your **user**

▶ Off-site, anytime access via Athens or referring URL
▶ Print or copy pages or chapters
▶ Full content search
▶ Bookmark, highlight and annotate text
▶ Access to thousands of pages of quality research
  at the click of a button

For more information, pricing enquiries or to order
a free trial, contact your local online sales team.

UK and Rest of World: **online.sales@tandf.co.uk**

US, Canada and Latin America:
e-reference@taylorandfrancis.com

www.ebooksubscriptions.com

ALPSP Award for
BEST eBOOK
PUBLISHER
2009 Finalist

Taylor & Francis eBooks
Taylor & Francis Group

A flexible and dynamic resource for teaching, learning and research.